Employee Complaint Handling

Recent Titles from Quorum Books

Judgment in International Accounting: A Theory of Cognition, Cultures, Language, and Contracts
Ahmed Belkaoui

The Evolution of Foreign Banking Institutions in the United States: Developments in International Finance
Faramarz Damanpour

Corporate Planning, Human Behavior, and Computer Simulation: Forecasting Business Cycles
Roy L. Nersesian

The Valuation and Investment Merits of Diamonds
Sarkis J. Khoury

Market-Oriented Pricing: Strategies for Management
Michael H. Morris and Gene Morris

The Divestiture Option:
A Guide for Financial and Corporate Planning Executives
Richard J. Schmidt

International Perspectives on Trade Promotion and Assistance
S. Tamer Cavusgil and Michael R. Czinkota, editors

The Promise of American Industry:
An Alternative Assessment of Problems and Prospects
Donald L. Losman and Shu-jan Liang

Global Corporate Intelligence: Opportunities, Technologies, and Threats in the 1990s
George S. Roukis, Hugh Conway, and Bruce Charnov, editors

The Process of Change in American Banking:
Political Economy and the Public Purpose
Jeremy F. Taylor

Drop Shipping as a Marketing Function:
A Handbook of Methods and Policies
Nicholas T. Scheel

Manufacturing for the Security of the United States:
Reviving Competitiveness and Reducing Deficits
Robert E. McGarrah

Employee Complaint Handling

TESTED TECHNIQUES FOR HUMAN RESOURCE MANAGERS

D. Keith Denton
and
Charles Boyd

Q

QUORUM BOOKS
New York • Westport, Connecticut • London

Library of Congress Cataloging-in-Publication Data

Denton, D. Keith.
Employee complaint handling : tested techniques for human resource managers / D. Keith Denton and Charles Boyd.
p. cm.
Includes bibliographical references.
ISBN 0-89930-433-8 (lib. bdg. : alk. paper)
1. Grievance procedures—United States. I. Boyd, Charles. II. Title.
HF5549.5.G7D46 1990
658.3'155—dc20 89-24371

British Library Cataloguing in Publication Data is available.

Library of Congress Catalog Card Number: 89-24371
ISBN: 0-89930-433-8

First published in 1990

Quorum Books, 88 Post Road West, Westport, CT 06881
An imprint of Greenwood Publishing Group, Inc.

Printed in the United States of America

∞

The paper used in this book complies with the Permanent Paper Standard issued by the National Information Standards Organization (Z39.48-1984).

10 9 8 7 6 5 4 3 2 1

To our families

Contents

Introduction

Employee Complaint Handling is a book designed for the human resource or personnel manager. Inside this book you will find a variety of techniques and tools that can be used to reduce the number of complaints and better manage those complaints that remain.

The book can be used as both a means of self instruction and as a training device to teach supervisors and staff how to better manage employee complaints. To this end, there are a variety of experiential learning exercises, roleplays, and case studies with helpful training notes. These techniques are also an effective way to improve self-learning.

The text material in this book is generally divided into two separate areas. The first four chapters and the learning exercises that follow provide the reader with a wide array of human relations and communication tools to better resolve complaints.

The last three chapters, learning exercises, and several cases at the end of the book focus on the legal and ethical side of complaint handling. This section examines critical issues facing managers in the area of race and sex discrimination as well as employment-at-will considerations. All of these time-tested techniques and tools are designed to help managers resolve employee complaints.

Chapter 5 augments these techniques with a potentially powerful new tool called peer review. This joint decision-making tool has been successfully used by General Electric to enhance its employee-management relationships and improve its employee complaint handling process. Chapter 5 looks at how they did it as well as the principles for setting up your own peer review system.

PART I

HUMAN RELATIONS AND COMMUNICATIONS

This section contains five chapters that examine how communication and human relations techniques can be used to prevent as well as manage employee complaints. Chapter 1 provides an overview of employee complaint handling, while chapters 2 through 4 provide specific techniques for better managing employee complaints. Chapter 5 reviews a relatively new and powerful technique called peer review.

The learning exercises at the end of this section can be used for self-instruction or as a means of training others in how to resolve employee complaints. It is wise to use exercise 1 before reviewing the other exercises since this exercise is designed to heighten awareness of the root problems of many employee complaints, namely poor listening skills. The remaining exercises in this section focus on ways of handling complaints after they occur and should be combined with lecture material in the previous chapters to train others to effectively resolve complaints.

1

Employee Complaints

Effective personnel managers handle employee complaints before they become formal grievances or cause serious performance or legal problems. Everyone, including personnel managers, hears them; some handle them better than others. To effectively handle complaints, you need to be able to recognize the most common types, understand their causes, and know how to resolve them.

Employee complaints are not necessarily bad, although many managers react that way. Some managers can even become irritated, afraid, or confused by them. They may feel the employee complaint is a reflection of their ability, but to the contrary, a reasonable number of complaints can indicate that managers are operating in an effective manner. Obviously something is seriously wrong if there is a flood of complaints, but some complaints are a natural outcome of the manager's relationship with the employees.

Much of chapter 1 originally appeared in the December 1987 issue of *Administrative Management* under the title of "Handling Employee Complaints Effectively."

RECOGNIZING COMPLAINTS

Employee complaints come in two forms—verbal and nonverbal. Almost everyone can recognize a verbal complaint, but recognizing nonverbal ones requires greater awareness. Personnel managers are missing a golden opportunity to improve relationships if they are not aware of nonverbal complaints. Nonverbal complaints are those destructive reactions by employees that allow the employee to retaliate upon you, another supervisor, or your company. They usually occur when employees feel they cannot get satisfaction by talking to you. Often they feel it is useless to talk because nothing will be done. Nonverbal complaints are thus frequently a way of reacting to work- and nonwork-related frustrations.

Employees who show an excessive number of absences; start to produce low quality products; become depressed, moody, or careless; or become discipline problems are often expressing their dissatisfaction nonverbally. Some other nonverbal complaints can include work slowdowns, horseplay, moonlighting, or even sleeping on the job. These actions can be an employee's way of complaining about some dissatisfaction. Unfortunately, many supervisors and personnel managers may not recognize these actions as an outcome of employee concerns. They simply say these problems are due to employee attitudes.

Alert managers, on the other hand, will recognize these nonverbal complaints and try to discover their causes. They will see these complaints as a chance to improve work performance. True, these managers and supervisors may receive more verbal complaints than do those who try to ignore them, but the intensity of those complaints will be less. The frequency may increase, but the severity will decrease. Being receptive may mean listening to more minor complaints, but ignoring them does not defuse them; it simply encourages employees to express their feelings in nonverbal ways.

REASONS FOR COMPLAINTS

Employee complaints occur for a wide variety of reasons. Some of the more common ones revolve around disciplinary action taken by managers. For instance, if you threaten employees with disciplinary action for being late to work, some may complain while others may even file formal grievances against the company. Other common complaints involve concern for promotions, layoffs, and the way the workload is distributed. For example, employees may complain about overtime because they think it is unnecessary or excessive.

All complaints should be treated seriously and with respect, but there is one that deserves special attention. Whenever an employee implies or accuses the company of discriminatory policies or of violating equal opportunity, there are special legal implications. Whenever this occurs, it is critical that you tell the employees it will be investigated and you will contact them at a specific time. Make sure you deliver on this promise, but it may be necessary to first consult someone in the legal department. This procedure in no way shows your ignorance nor is it a way of shifting responsibility. With all the legal complications that can occur in discrimination cases, it is critical that expert counsel be obtained. A typical manager cannot be expected to be qualified to handle such legally sensitive areas.

Some complaints can be very serious, but even the simplest ones may be more serious than you might think at first. Employee dissension cannot always be taken at face value. True, some employees may complain that the pay, overtime, or discipline is unfair, but these complaints may not accurately tell you what is wrong. People do not always tell you directly what is bothering them. Employees can complain about the working conditions or pay when what is really dissatisfying them may be the belief that you have favorites. They might also complain about overtime when what is really troubling them is a personal problem or a bad night's sleep. Of course, it is not wise to pry into their personal lives, but you must understand their motives if you hope to resolve the complaints.

UNDERSTANDING YOUR EMPLOYEES

To effectively analyze complaints, you must understand human nature and, in particular, your employees' and supervisors' motives. You must be able to see what life is dealing them and what they think is important. If you want to reduce or defuse complaints, make a point of being interested in what your supervisors and employees are doing. Find out what they want, but avoid giving advice on personal matters. It is always best to encourage your employees to reflect on matters for themselves.

Never assume there are no serious complaints just because you have not heard them. Frequently this is done because of limited contact with and knowledge about employees, and because managers believe their employees have little knowledge of work matters. This attitude is wrong more often than not; but, more importantly, it establishes a poor environment between managers and their employees. While your employees may not have a detailed understanding of why something cannot be done, never assume they are ignorant or naive. This attitude only increases employee resentment and leads to more complaints. It takes only a few ignored complaints to convince others that you do not take them or their opinions seriously.

Explaining your point of view will go a long way toward improving your relationship with employees. In turn, improved relationships help reduce the minor complaints that often arise at work. Do not assume the facts are obvious; they are probably obvious only to you. Encourage employees to speak up if they have questions or complaints. Simply encouraging them to do this often reduces the frequency and severity of complaints. Sometimes people want someone to listen to their side more than they actually expect action. Relationships are also improved and complaints reduced when you try to understand their points of view. If you make a mistake, admit it and take corrective action if possible. Do not defend poor choices or stall about taking action. Correcting errors reduces complaints; defending poor decisions increases them.

EMPLOYEE PERSPECTIVE

Managing complaints, like so many other aspects of management, takes awareness. Putting yourself mentally in someone else's shoes is a good place to start. Take your employees' perspective. If you were working under their conditions and dealing with their work and personal problems, what would your reaction be? Do not treat complaints as trivial—they are not trivial to your employees. Exercise 2 (Resolving Complaints Through Communication) at the end of this section can be used as a learning tool to show participants how to evaluate the negative as well as positive aspects of communication.

Expect complaints because you are in a position to receive them. Your decisions often have a major impact on the organization because they become the accepted practice of dealing with employees. They establish precedents. As the person in charge you will often be expected to interpret labor contracts and policies immediately. For this reason, it is essential to have an exact understanding of what each contract clause means. If no labor contract exists, then understand specifically what the accepted or past practice has been. Be aware of setting precedents. Case study number 5 (Management Persuasion of Potential Union Members) at the end of the book demonstrates how precedents can lead to complaints and even legal problems for an organization. Union or nonunion management actions and behavior toward employees can result in intentional or unintentional discrimination. Regardless of the intent, the result is the same—trouble.

Avoiding dangerous precedents is never easy, but it becomes impossible if you do not plan ahead. Have forethought, and inquire before the crisis occurs. If necessary, get the advice of experts on such matters as coffee breaks, leaves of absence, lunch periods, or any other policy of which you are unsure. Make sure you are certain of your actions before you take them. If you do not know the correct procedure, review the company manual, policies, and procedures before acting. Be prepared. Such an approach builds your reputation as a consistent and fair manager. If others perceive you as fair and consistent, you will have fewer complaints.

EXPLAIN WORK RULES TO EMPLOYEES

This is obvious, but it is sometimes overlooked. Employees will complain if they do not know the work rules. Management's responsibility is to inform employees—repeatedly if necessary—of company rules, regulations, and standard operating procedures. Friendly reminders are essential if adherence to rules becomes lax. If you counsel employees before you take disciplinary action you will have fewer complaints.

No one likes to keep written records, but it is essential since some decisions may result in legal challenges. Written records document your past actions. Records will be especially valuable if you are ever asked to justify those actions. Written records can have a significant impact on whether your decision is overturned or not. They also help show that you were consistent and nondiscriminatory. Even your best employees will appeal some of your decisions if they feel these decisions were unfair. Written support is always better than verbal or hearsay information—so keep records, documents, and notes on discussions that take place.

INVESTIGATE COMPLAINTS

The degree of investigation will vary with the seriousness of the complaint, but always determine the specifics of the complaint. As already noted, there may be underlying causes to what first appear to be obvious complaints. For this reason, any action against employees should be clearly supported by facts. Their work records should be part of the investigation.

When possible, all complaints should be settled promptly. Early settlements save time and money, and increase employees' confidence in you. Early settlements also gain your own supervisor's confidence.

Many employees will also think you are indecisive if you fail to act within a reasonable period of time. Early settlements help prevent minor complaints from becoming major problems. All employees are entitled to know your response. If a complaint requires interviewing others, make sure to tell them you will contact them with an answer—and do it.

CONTROL EMOTIONS

Emotional outbursts impede problem solving. If an employee disagrees, the worst possible action is to start a shouting match. Talking down to employees or other emotional reactions prevent constructive problem solving. Even if an employee seems to want to start an argument or put you on the defensive, do not let it happen. If an employee insists on shouting or getting into a verbal argument, terminate the meeting, and set it up for some other time. A calmer setting may lead to more rational thinking.

In many cases listening will serve you well. When employees complain, take the time to listen to them. When they complain they are probably tense, so let them talk. It can be difficult to put concerns into logical phrases.

Do not correct the complaining employee's minor incorrect statement. You may have to correct it later, but wait until the employee has finished an emotional outburst. If you have to correct the employee's misunderstanding, make sure to do so without humiliation or embarrassment.

EXPLAIN DECISIONS CLEARLY

If possible, when answering employee complaints, make every effort to give clear and direct answers. Provide specific reasons for why something can or cannot be done. Below is an example of how one company, using its formal procedures, effectively handled a complaint by one group of employees.

> Concerning Vacation Time, we in Final Inspection were told that we could only take 5 single vacation days a year. We were also told that if we take a vacation day on a Friday and are scheduled to work Saturday, we have to come in and work that Saturday, rather than have the weekend off. After talking to people in other departments, we're finding out they can take as many vacation days as they want a year, and take a vacation day on Friday and get the whole weekend off, scheduled or not.
> This is unfair, we are a company, and if rules are made, they should be carried out plant wide, not by department.

The response from Personnel, as seen in the response below, was specific and detailed.

> This letter is in response to your request dated May 24, 1989. In regard to the five single vacation days per year, our vacation policy reads as follows: Employees may, however, be granted vacation in daily increments (up to 5 days per anniversary year) with the following provisions:
>
> a. The employee must have a compelling personal reason.
> b. The employee understands that vacation pay will not be made in advance.
> c. The arrangement is compatible with the work requirements of the department.
> d. The vacation is approved on or before the actual days on vacation.
>
> It is the supervisor's responsibility to have the number of employees needed to satisfy the overtime requirement. Therefore, if the department is required to work on Saturday and you take a vacation day on Friday, and do not work on Saturday, this arrangement is not compatible with the work requirements of the department, as in provision c above of the policy. We will look at the other departments and see what needs to be done to enforce the policy in the other departments.

If you have any other questions, do not hesitate to contact me.

Avoid such statements as "It's company policy," or "It's upper management's decision," or "No!" Communicate clearly the reasons for your decision, especially if it is not in the employee's favor. Whenever you give answers, make sure employees understand what you have said, and make sure you understand what they have said. Paraphrase in your own words what you think they have said.

This process enhances understanding. At the very least it shows that you are really listening! Psychologically it also helps to establish a positive climate because at least you begin to agree on some points. This process also aids objective problem solving.

KEEP YOUR PROMISES

Although the value of following through on promises is self-evident, many managers still make promises they cannot keep. There is a tendency to do this when dealing with an emotionally upset employee. Resist this temptation, and make sure you can do what you say you can. Broken promises destroy credibility and increase the severity of complaints. Identify the problem, define the cause, and show employees that you appreciate their trouble, but do not spontaneously tell them you will do something that you cannot accomplish.

Complaints occur; it is how they are handled that makes the difference. Do not try to suppress them, or they will resurface in destructive ways (e.g., lower productivity). When investigating complaints, do not take every comment at face value. You will be better able to understand the causes and find solutions if you understand your employees' needs and motives. Discover what each employee needs.

When complaints do occur, try to resolve them at the earliest opportunity. Time has a way of increasing their severity. The longer the time, the more serious complaints generally become. In discussing complaints, try to find a place that provides privacy and a calm climate.

When discussing criticism, make a point of showing that you are giving your undivided attention. It helps to paraphrase and summarize complaints to make sure you and your employee both understand each other. Listen, encourage, be open, admit mistakes, but do not make promises you cannot keep.

Personnel managers constantly face complaints from a variety of personnel and for a variety of reasons. They must deal directly with employees who have complaints. While handling volatile situations is a part of every manager's job, the focus should be on prevention. Preventative measures like supervisory training should be a part of every personnel manager's job.

2

Creating an Atmosphere for Resolving Complaints

To effectively manage complaints involving superiors, employees, and peers, it is important to establish a cooperative atmosphere between yourself and others. Before examining ways of managing these complaints we need to emphasize several don'ts.

When a complaint first arises many managers mistakenly approach the complaining person or those who are being complained about and demand some action. Phrases such as, "You have to . . . !" are often perceived as an overt threat and fail to win much cooperation in resolving the complaint. A similar counterproductive threatening phrase would be, "You better not . . ." These types of statements are made by a person with a strong ego but little understanding of other people's feelings. Statements such as, "You ought to do this . . . ," or "Why don't you . . ." can cause others to become defensive and resist new ideas or methods of solving the problem. Obviously, much resentment and lack of cooperation in resolving the complaint occurs when others feel as though they are being placed in a win/lose situation. Flat or blunt responses such as "You're wrong," "That was dumb," or "You've totally misunderstood the whole thing!" can create immediate disputes and confrontations instead of cooperation.

One of the best ways to solve the problem is through the use of

"I messages." Instead of mistakenly placing the blame on someone else, as emphasized by these "you messages," you can use "I messages" combined with descriptive words and personal feelings. These three elements are all necessary to gain cooperation. Frequently, people will start a conversation with an I message, but fail to accept their responsibility. The result is still an ineffective approach. A typical situation is one in which someone starts the conversation with an I message, but then ends up evaluating another's behavior. For example, an evaluation message would be, "I can't help if you are so thoughtless that you don't do your part." This same statement projected in a descriptive tone, instead of interjecting the unproductive evaluation, would be, "I can't help if you don't complete your part." Combining the I message and descriptive words in the previous statement with an expression of your own personal feelings is the most effective approach. Such an approach is demonstrated as follows: "I am very concerned about being able to (I message) (personal feelings) resolve this problem and need . . ." (descriptive words).

This is the most effective approach because you are not placing blame on someone else. The other person also knows how you feel and will not feel defensive since the condition was described in an unthreatening manner. Since the other person does not feel as defensive, resistance is reduced and cooperation is increased. Such an approach provides the other person with subtle information about some desired behavior but does not evaluate that behavior. However, maybe the best advantage of such an approach is that it shows other people you are being open and honest.

LISTENING TO THE CONTENT AND CONTEXT

Once you accept the responsibility to resolve complaints, you are obligated to become involved in the process. This primarily requires that you listen to both the content and the feelings of a message. Concentrating on these two characteristics helps clarify what others are saying. This concentration is especially important when you do not like the person who is sending the message. The more judgmental, evaluative, and self-centered someone is, the less likely he will be able to listen effectively.

In a general sense, effective listening is being able to openly listen to others without a great deal of energy placed on your own point of view. Specifically, to be able to listen effectively to the content and feelings of messages means improving your perceptual process. This involves having the skill to effectively send, receive, and understand verbal and nonverbal messages.

If the meanings of the words everyone uses were the same, there would be no problems in communicating. If we also only used words that described tangible objects such as hat, chair, and so on, then there would be little disagreement about their meanings. We could simply point to the object in question and resolve the disagreement over the meaning of the word. However, adults must deal in abstract concepts and words that describe such concepts that have a wide range of meanings. Each person will have a different definition for words like *love*, *truth*, *freedom*, *efficiency*, and so on. It is difficult to point to one set of experiences or situations in the hope of clarifying what is meant by a specific word. Likewise, even the meanings we attach to words vary from generation to generation (for example, *nice* one meant unaware). Since language constantly changes, it is everyone's responsibility to keep an updated dictionary and make a practice of defining the meanings of words that might cause misunderstanding.

Meanings of words also vary from situation to situation and from one group of people to the next. Try to avoid the tendency to listen to a few sentences and believe someone is complaining about something. Instead, evaluate the person's logic and underlying reasons for making such statements.

The various meanings that we have for the same word are the direct result of our past associations and experiences with the word. To some degree, everyone perceives a different meaning for a wide range of words. In some cases the meanings that one group attaches to words can be dramatically different from your own meanings. For instance, the word *report* can mean something entirely different to a mechanical engineer, a computer specialist, and a first-line supervisor. Similarly, if you want to set up a program to motivate another group of people, the meaning of *motivate* for others may range from authoritarian to democratic images.

Whenever possible, avoid the use of vague generalities and instead use concrete language and specific details. The use of jargon that excludes someone who is not in your special group also increases misunderstanding. While jargon or spoken shorthand is necessary and useful, it can be overused when talking to another manager who is not part of your department. Personnel managers are especially prone to cause this unintentional misunderstanding but can avoid it by recognizing that there are people within the organization who do not understand their jargon.

Depending on your past experiences, the words you use can carry either positive, negative, or neutral values. Typical words that have varying associations for different groups of employees are *unions*, *top management*, *college graduate*, and *promotion.* Effective listening helps you decide what type of language is most appropriate for the situation.

Whenever you use words that have either a positive or negative emotionally charged meaning, it is referred to as connotative language. Connotative words include *bigot*, *manipulate*, *brainwash*, *dominate*, *stupid*, or any number of taboo words. Connotative words are not always bad or good. Writers of fiction and poetry make use of these words, as do any writers who wish to appeal to someone's emotions and gain his support. Connotative words always involve value judgments.

If you are interested in giving only facts, use denotative language, which involves using words that are not emotionally charged. These neutral words contain little, if any, negative or positive evaluative meanings. Some of these words would include *manage* instead of *manipulate* or *train* instead of *brainwash.* Whenever you must get cooperation, avoid frequent reference to words that produce a strong negative emotional reaction. Similarly, you would seek to use positively associated words.

Just because some group has a negative association with some words does not mean this situation must always exist. There is evidence that suggests that providing new associations for a word can change the response to the word. During the verbal listening process, you should seek to isolate words to which someone has a negative association. For instance, if someone has negative associations with some aspect of accounting, engineering, or designing, then you would seek to change the association to a more positive one. Associating aspects of your department or function with rewarding and enriching experiences is only one way of changing these associations. In sending verbal messages, you would associate yourself with activities that make other people feel good about their own abilities as well as your own abilities. Techniques would include, but are not limited to, recognition of others' contributions, encouraging participation in problem-solving opportunities, and trusting others' opinions. Avoiding misunderstandings and improving your chances of obtaining cooperation require a knowledge of someone else's definitions of the words they use. It also involves associating yourself with the most positively reinforcing words and actions.

Another aspect involves the accuracy of your communications. The primary way of improving the accuracy of communication is by isolating factual and inferential statements. A statement such as "I am sure they will be against that . . ." is an inferential statement, unless the speaker has reliable facts to verify that conclusion. While some inferential statements are harmless, others can generate complaints and problems. This can occur when you hear and believe someone else is against you even if there is no truth to the statements. When a negative inferential statement is made, it is up to you to find the facts before assuming that you have a conflict. Likewise, when preparing to investigate a complaint, you should not believe you have another person's understanding unless you verify the commitment. Statements such as "I am sure that they will agree to . . ." are statements that should not be accepted as fact until you have investigated the situation. Initially, this verifying process may take up more time, but it has the advantage of providing accurate information. The end result includes being better able to prevent disagreements and increase cooperation.

Along with emphasizing sending and listening for accurate information, you can improve the probability of cooperation by avoiding rigid classifications of people and situations. Although people often view someone as being either good or bad or being for or against them, this is rarely the case. In most cases, another person's feelings, attitudes, and interests more closely resemble a continuum. In general, all people are alike, but the psychological and physical characteristics of each individual show an amazing range. There are no purely good or evil people, but some have more positive characteristics than others do. You do not have arch enemies, only people who disagree with you to some extent.

Although everyone has a classification system, it is important to avoid classifying someone as an opposite or adversary since this produces a strong tendency to create resistance and solidify opposition. If you view another person as having some differences with you, but not as diametrically opposite, cooperation is more likely. Once you recognize shades of differences, you can begin to seek common ground. The philosophy moves from "me against them" to "us." Instead of winning or losing, it is a balanced and rational approach. The best way of accomplishing rationality is to continually seek to isolate the degree of meaning to which others agree or disagree. A statement such as "To what degree do you . . ." is an example of isolating common ground.

Listening is also improved by isolating and adjusting to the social language patterns of each culture, group, or occupation. In some situations, such as in the judicial system, the verbal patterns are very formal and educated. In other cases, the language is less formal and less "correct," with the use of a great deal of slang. Cooperation comes more easily if you learn to speak the language that is accepted by a particular group. In many cases, as in discussions with a less-educated person, this means learning to speak the dialect of the region. If you are going to live and work in the northern or southern United States, then you should learn to speak the appropriate northern or southern dialect, since the "correct" pronunciation varies from region to region.

Cooperation can be improved when you pay attention to communication between yourself and others. This is often difficult for many people, but with practice you can become quite good at this process. Putting aside other tasks to focus on the matter at hand at once improves your ability. Recognizing that you often have biased feelings that interfere with what you perceive someone else is saying can also be an advantage to effective verbal communication. It is natural to be offended when someone communicates in a manner that challenges your values or goals. However, you should at least attempt to look beyond your impulsive feelings and try to understand what point is being made. This realization can create an atmosphere of cooperation and negotiation. Specifically, you can increase cooperation in resolving complaints by applying the following principles:

1. understand the meanings of someone else's words
2. improve the accuracy of the communication process (this involves emphasizing key points, reflecting on your and others' feelings, and paraphrasing when necessary)
3. avoid rigid classifications
4. learn to adjust to different social language patterns

DESTRUCTIVE ACTIONS THAT CREATE COMPLAINTS

Whenever you react in a threatening or defensive manner you increase the probability of serious complaints. The following are specific actions that create threats and/or defensive responses and increase the likelihood of complaints.

1. *Limiting the number of ways to communicate.* (Talking by itself will not reduce complaints, but the lack of communication can be a barrier to resolving them.)
2. *When complaining individuals or groups make poor use of the communication channels available.* (If employees can only communicate at specific times and through limited means, for example, written or verbal, then it is even

more critical to be prepared and have reasoned out the options available.)

3. *Attempting to limit communication between disagreeing people.* (When complaints occur, you should make the communication more productive, not less frequent.)
4. *Failing to empathize with another person.* (Understanding another's point of view will help you address the concerns of the other person.)
5. *Failing to exactly state the position of the other person.* (Each needs to understand what is being said, not what he thinks was said.)
6. *Unintentionally or intentionally creating feelings of hostility in each other.* (Hostility not only creates complaints but it widens and deepens their impact.)
7. *Rejecting a third (neutral) person's involvement when a deadlock is reached.* (Complaints are solidified when compromise is not an option.)
8. *Trying to impose preconceived solutions through power.* (Energy is spent developing and promoting a strategy of outwitting others instead of seeking cooperation.)

Many complaints are caused by ineffective interpersonal communication, a lack of understanding and appreciation of each other, and ineffective problem solving. Complaints continue to grow when defensive responses block clear thinking and when a cold, threatening environment exists between two people or groups. Complaints also develop because each party does not emphasize a problem-solving approach to settling disagreements. To effectively use a problem-solving approach, one must remain flexible about resolving complaints.

METHODS OF MANAGING COMPLAINTS

To successfully manage complaints, personnel managers must concentrate on understanding and controlling what is being communicated. For instance, if you make it clear through verbal statements or actions that you do not share another individual's attitudes or values, then complaints may result in more serious grievances.

Complaints are likely to decrease when there is an open and trusting environment, but there are times when complete honesty can create disagreements. While you need not lie, there are situations where specific attitudes and feelings need not be expressed. Reminding a noncollege graduate of one's own degree or a deeply religious person of one's neutrality are typical examples of information that need not be volunteered. Undercutting an employee's self-esteem by "honestly" pointing out his or her mistakes, ignorance, flaws, or inexperience creates more serious problems.

To successfully manage complaints you must complete four tasks. The first task is to establish an environment that is conducive to controlling and settling complaints. Primarily, this consists of de-emphasizing the win/lose attitude common to complaints. Second, you must be able to project a good attitude toward others so that they will want to solve the problem. It is not enough to have attitudes that product a cooperative atmosphere, you must know how to display your good attitude so others can recognize it. Third, you must seek ways of reducing present complaints to their simplest form so that each is more manageable. The fourth and final task is to manage the complaints that remain so that there are long-term solutions to them.

DE-EMPHASIZING THE WIN/LOSE ATTITUDE

In managing complaints, your first task must always be to emphasize a cooperative atmosphere. Embodied within this approach is the elimination of the win/lose attitude that intensifies complaints. You need to avoid thinking of the situation in terms of winning or losing, even though this perception is difficult to ignore. Although employees may be trying to obtain a concession for themselves, a personnel manager who emphasizes a cooperative atmosphere will want to keep the need for victory out of the minds of the complainers. Admittedly this is a difficult but essential task if problems are to be solved. At times this can appear even more difficult than usual when an employee is angry and dominated by hostile feelings. During these emotionally charged times, the best advice may be to restrain your destructive feelings until the rational mind regains control over the situation. Regardless of the method used, it is imperative that you avoid hostile outbursts since they prevent the exchange of information between people. Without an open dialogue between people, a win/lose perspective will very likely dominate.

To prevent employees from being dominated by those negative feelings that destroy open dialogue, you must be aware of the obsessive and repeated justification of these destructive feelings. In time, most personnel can gain some understanding of someone else's point of view if they do not keep thinking, "I have a right to feel this way!" or "That would make anyone mad!" There is no need to rationalize these negative emotional feelings since the real problem is to arrive at solutions, not justify anger. You can more easily arrive at solutions to complaints if there is little emphasis put on their origin.

In addition to not justifying negative feelings, each of the following techniques is designed to de-emphasize a win/lose attitude that often exists between disagreeing parties. The first technique that you can use for avoiding a win/lose environment between personnel is to emphasize common goals. Instead of telling someone why he or she needs to accomplish a task or why someone needs to cooperate, the approach should be one of joint collaboration. To emphasize collaboration, the personnel manager must ask and answer the following question: "What common goals does the complaining person share with the others?" Usually these goals revolve around economic and productivity objectives. Reminding others of overall goals is an effective collaboration technique.

One should be as specific as possible about common goals. Abstract reference to common goals is a fairly easy task, but the best motivational goals are those that are concrete and specific. A statement that specifically identifies common goals could be stated as, "This is our task, and these are the things that must be done before we can achieve our objective." As in the previous statement, you will need to emphasize "us," "we," "ours" instead of "mine" or "my" if the focus is to be on common objectives and goals. Emphasizing common goals not only helps resolve present complaints, it also helps prevent future ones.

The second technique used to de-emphasize win/lose thinking has to do with recognizing mutually beneficial rewards for each party's collaboration. Reminding others of shared rewards that occur when a task is completed can be a powerful motivational tool. Providing a list of specific promotion, monetary, status, influence, and recognition rewards that are likely outcomes of mutually completing the task helps keep the atmosphere one of partnership. The accent must be on positive outcomes that can occur due to the resolution of the complaint by reaching some agreement.

Showing a willingness to achieve shared goals is a significant way of settling complaints. Explaining the need to preserve a relationship is one way to build the trust needed to avoid win/lose thinking. Making yourself easily accessible to others and freely providing information are other ways of demonstrating this willingness to achieve shared goals.

Stressing the urgency of the task is a final technique that can be used. Most people will procrastinate when matters do not seem urgent. There is an even greater tendency to procrastinate when difficult decisions must be made. On the other hand, if stress is placed on resolving the situation by a specific date, then collaboration is more likely. Reference to specific management directives and establishing target dates are ways of noting the importance of completing the task on time. Another way is by explaining how a delay in resolving the complaint can lead to other delays.

DISPLAYING CONSTRUCTIVE PERSONALITY ATTRIBUTES

Certain personality characteristics, such as narrow-mindedness, increase the risk of disputes. On the other hand, there are attitudes that help resolve disagreements before they become complaints.

Before we review these, consider the following situation: Jan, a production supervisor; Sam, a stores clerk; and Ralph, a warehouse assistant, are discussing the use of a new computer system that is currently being implemented. They and others are trying to develop a compatible system. Just before the meeting, Marsha, Ralph's close friend, told him "Jan is such a squirrel. I've heard she'd like to use the new computer program to take over the inventory system." As the meeting started, the following conversation took place:

Sam: You know, everyone around here is never going to go for this system they're trying to implement.

Jan: Yeah! It's going to be a pain, but we've got to do it. (small talk between all three)

Ralph: Well, I don't know about you guys, but I think we've got to have more time to debug the system before we can get it up and running.

Sam: Well, if you ask me, I think we should wait until the 1st to start this. I really don't have time right now to fool with this. (all concur)

Jan: I'm going to need my own computer terminal or else this whole discussion, from my point of view, is a waste of time.

Ralph: (interrupting Jan) Do you think you're the only one that needs the terminal!! (bickering between Jan and Ralph)

Jan: As I mentioned before, I don't know about the rest of you, but my department has to have the third software package we reviewed. (irritated comments from the other two)

Sam: I think you're being petty about that. If you keep this up you're wasting my time.

All three of these supervisors are demonstrating destructive attitudes that prevent any solutions. Problems are certain to occur unless someone takes charge. Sam's unnecessary opinions and judgments are hindering their progress. Likewise, Ralph's negative attitude (maybe due to his distrust of Jan) and Jan's insistence on only thinking about the problem from her point of view increase the likelihood of serious conflicts.

There are certain personality characteristics that increase the risk of complaints, as well as personality attributes that help resolve them.

One characteristic that can be very beneficial in helping to manage complaints is to avoid judgments of others' actions. In discussions about some disagreement you should avoid criticizing an employee's behavior because it creates a feeling of defensiveness. In our example, unless Jan is a superior person, Sam's criticism of her by calling her petty will probably lead to a hostile attitude.

Defensiveness is an attitude that prevents settlements since one is afraid of doing or saying anything that will damage oneself in some way. If the disagreeing person feels that he or she will be held responsible for their past errors, then each will avoid taking any action that might damage their credibility, and this especially includes creatively seeking new ways of handling complaints. If the personnel manager, either verbally or mentally, seeks to place the blame on someone for a past act that that person cannot change, then little rational problem solving can occur. Typical statements that imply these types of destructive judgments would include, "You got yourself into this, so what are you going to do about it?" or "Why didn't you do this?" Each one of these and other judgmental statements will generate fear and defensiveness in others and should be avoided.

Empathy, or the vicarious sharing of another's emotions and feelings, is an action that helps each party reach an understanding and agreement. Being sensitive to another person's feelings can prevent as well as settle complaints. This was not the attitude that Jan had in the above example when she kept insisting on only looking at the problem from her point of view. It is not enough for the personnel manager to believe that he or she understands an employee's problem; the employee must be shown that the manager really does understand and appreciate those feelings. For empathy to be useful in settling complaints, you must demonstrate an appreciation for the employee's viewpoint. For instance, it is often necessary to state that you find the employee's proposal or views to be unacceptable. While this must be done, it should always be stated in a manner that emphasizes your concern for the employee's viewpoint. Some techniques for doing this are discussed in the feedback tools section in chapter 3, but there are several considerations that can be mentioned now.

For example, you can remain open and considerate. A simple statement like, "As I understand it, this is how you feel. . . . However, this is where I am having a problem with this approach . . ." can show your consideration. Another way of showing consideration is to simply avoid interrupting someone who is expressing his or her feelings. Even if you think you know what that person is going to say, it is vital to avoid interrupting him or her. When you allow others to express themselves, you increase the possibility that the others will also be empathetic and let you express yourself. In turn, you are more likely to become more considerate of each other's feelings and place a greater value on that person's opinion even when it is difficult or painful to do so.

Honesty and trust are positive attributes that aid in managing complaints. The most difficult challenge is to be honest with someone by freely admitting any mistakes that were made. However, this is necessary whenever you recognize or know of your organization's mistake. Trying to deny or hide a mistake will lead to bitter disagreement and mistrust. The employee's logic is, "If they lied this time, how can I believe anything they say?"

As the competitive or win/lose environment becomes more severe, it will become increasingly difficult to be honest with a complaining party, but the effort needs to be made. One way of gradually building up your image as an honest person is through the sharing of relevant information. This means freely providing information that is available and relevant to the complaint even if it does not completely support your own viewpoint.

Making an extra effort to verify your information and citing the sources is also a way of displaying honesty. Identifying any bias that the information may contain will greatly increase your reputation. Whenever it is impossible to be totally honest and admit personal mistakes (as is sometimes the case in highly emotional situations), you should at least be honest about the information supporting your position. In the long run, exposing any temporary weakness or flaw in your supporting information can be of tremendous benefit. Through this type of unbiased action you develop a reputation as an honest person.

The gradual development of this reputation will more than compensate you in the form of increased trust and respect from peers and other personnel. Trust is a quality that comes from being honest with others and is not easily acquired, but it is well worth the effort. It also comes from demonstrating a commitment and dependability to work at settling the complaint and meeting your obligations. Personnel managers who concentrate on building a reputation as dependable, honest, and trustworthy problem solvers will experience fewer and less severe complaints than those who look at the short-term rewards of deceit and manipulation of others for personal gain.

Giving positive reinforcement can also help prevent win/lose attitudes. Positive reinforcement not only improves the cooperative environment, but it also helps eliminate complaints that already exist. Recognizing someone's valuable contributions is one example of positive reinforcement. If a person makes a helpful statement or suggests a beneficial idea, that person should be rewarded in the form of additional recognition or even by giving them greater responsibility in solving the problem. Positive reinforcement can be a simple statement such as, "That's a good idea, do you know of another way we could use it?"

In the previous case no one made any positive reinforcing comments despite the opportunity to do so. When Ralph mentioned wanting to wait until the first of the month, someone could have said something like, "Well, that's a good idea. Why don't we start working toward that date to make some of our major decisions, but before that we need to get some facts on . . . ." Likewise, when Jan noted that she needed her own computer terminal someone could have said, "I think you're right—you probably need your own terminal and so will some others. Let's see if we can decide how many terminals we'll need." Jan also mentioned that she preferred the third software package. Someone could have built on that by saying, "Yes, we need to look at all the software packages to decide which will work best for all of us—maybe we could use the best aspect of several packages."

In any discussion, there are times when someone does something constructive, is particularly helpful, or encourages rational thinking. These are the times to recognize and acknowledge that helpful advice. A positively reinforcing individual will make a practice of rewarding others in these situations and ignoring, as much as possible, the same individual's negative comments. If you avoid giving attention to negative comments, then these comments will diminish over time. It is up to you to concentrate on recognizing the positive inputs of others and de-emphasizing or ignoring the hostile and win/lose comments. The end result will be a more positive and cooperative feeling among all parties.

All of these constructive personality attributes are interrelated. Each one contributes to and builds support for the other characteristics. Each of these can reduce the emotionalism of many complaints as well as eliminate potential complaints. Others must see tangible evidence that you are honest, trustworthy, and positively reinforcing. Being committed to solving the problem at hand, considering the feelings of others, being open-minded, and supplying relevant information are ways of constructively establishing a good complaint-solving atmosphere.

Complaints can more easily be resolved or prevented when the personnel manager develops a cooperative atmosphere. Establishing this atmosphere requires that you listen to the total message being communicated, including what was meant as well as what was said. To this end, it is helpful to focus on using concrete language and providing as many details as possible.

Attitude is also important. Avoid rigid classifications and seek degrees of agreement. Other methods for establishing this cooperative atmosphere include:

- avoid destructive actions (i.e., limit the number of ways to communicate, etc.)
- de-emphasize the win/lose attitudes
- emphasize honesty and trust
- use positive reinforcement
- recognize others' valuable contributions

3

Resolving Complaints

The previous methods for managing complaints involved establishing an environment and projecting attitudes that help settle disagreements. The next two methods will aid in managing any complaint even though they are most effective when the previous methods have been implemented. Under any situation you will want to first reduce the complaint to its simplest form. This means reducing the ego or emotionally charged aspect of complaints to the more manageable and rational level. It is these basic and rational complaints that are more easily managed through rational problem solving. Emotional complaints are nurtured by hostility and suspicion. Therefore, implementing the suggestions in chapter 2 will help reduce the emotionalism of these complaints, though even in the least corrosive atmosphere, emotional outbursts will occur.

Consider how a manager might resolve complaints in order to reduce workplace hazards. Al, the safety manager, has recently introduced a new safety system involving a great deal more inspection. Sam, a production supervisor working on piece rate, is very unhappy. He feels that the new safety system wastes his time and hinders production. He paces into Al's office.

Sam: (frowning) Al, your new inspection system is a real

pain! We can't have safety inspectors always over here stopping the line! I've got production quotas to meet!

Al: (irritated) We've all got safety standards to meet! You ought to know safety is our first consideration.

Sam: I know you've got standards, but your people are getting in the way.

Al: You should concentrate on following the rules, not on watching my people.

Sam: I've had it! I intend to let Sara (personnel manager) know about this. Things have got to change!

Al: Go ahead! She'll just tell you what I've already said. Safety first.

Do you think this situation was properly handled? What would you have done if Sam had walked into your office?

One technique that can be used to reduce this emotionalism to a manageable level is to listen more and talk less. In an emotional situation there is a strong tendency for each party to become highly self-centered and not consider others' viewpoints. As a result of this perspective, the discussion between the parties becomes less and less beneficial. It is during these emotional outbursts that the reasoning mind is lost and statements are made that will solidify resistance and create deep resentment.

To avoid making statements that you might regret and to help others maintain a calm manner, it is wise to simply reduce the amount of talking since no dialogue is taking place. In this type of discussion there is a strong tendency to try to stifle the other person by talking too much. This tendency should be avoided since it only serves destructive purposes. Conversely, when you give each person respectful consideration by listening, there is a high probability that they will give you and eventually each other the same courtesy. Since calm and rational discussion leads to solutions, it is wise to listen.

As in the above example, sometimes disagreements degenerate to the point that each party becomes excessively emotional. Since calm dialogue will be necessary before disagreements are resolved, it may be necessary to avoid these emotional discussions for a short period of time. Delaying discussion allows each party time to calm down so that rational thinking is possible. The delay provides time for you to analyze what went wrong in the first place. You can also try to avoid thinking about the personal attacks that were made and concentrate on creatively exploring new alternatives or solutions. Finally, you can spend the time collecting information that might be needed when discussion resumes. The activity should focus on problem solving, not getting upset over the disagreeable aspects of someone's personality.

MANAGING COMPLAINTS THAT REMAIN

Up to this point several considerations have been identified that help prevent complaints. The previous chapter emphasized the need for honesty, trust, empathy, and treating others as equals if complaints are to be prevented. Likewise, you must understand that your own defensive responses can block the settlement of complaints. After addressing these issues and reducing the complaint to its simplest form, it only remains for you to clarify any remaining distortion or fallacies and arrive at a mutually satisfactory solution to the problem.

The odds of reaching a final agreement will increase if you keep three objectives in mind. First, you must convey the message to your personnel in a nonthreatening manner. Second, it is equally important for all parties involved to develop an accurate understanding of the message being communicated. Last, you must use a rational, problem-solving approach to complaint handling.

The techniques described below were designed with these objectives clearly in mind. Each is a practical aid in bringing the complaint into focus and together they provide personnel managers with a rational scheme for solving complaints in an incremental manner until the whole disagreement has been resolved. Needless to say, while these techniques have the potential for eliminating disputes, their usefulness will depend on the ability of the manager.

If you practice using these techniques, you can develop a high degree of skill in preventing as well as settling disputes.

CLARIFYING SOLUTIONS

Clarifying solutions means promoting an understanding between both parties about the nature of the complaint by isolating what is needed and what must be done to solve the problem. Focus is placed on seeking solutions, not dwelling on causes. To resolve complaints, you must avoid spending time seeking causes of the present difficulty. Dwelling on causes means that the vast amount of your time and energy is spent placing blame, not seeking solutions. Searching for causes can only prevent future complaints; it will not solve the present one. Once the problem is solved there will be plenty of time to prevent future ones.

It is important to note that there are two questions that should not be asked since they will produce complaints, not settle them. The first taboo question is, "Who caused this problem?" This question can quickly consume a discussion between disagreeing parties and is in fact a sign of the most severe complaint. Placing blame will never isolate the cause of disputes; it will only divert attention from problem solving. Another question that should not be asked in one-on-one discussion is, "What caused the problem?" Again, you are spending time in the past when the real solution is in future thinking.

Clarifying solutions involves coming to some agreement on four very specific problem-solving questions. The first question that must be answered is, "What is the complaint about?" Agreeing on a simple statement about the complaint is necessary before other specifics can be discussed. Often this is a simple process and may involve a statement like, "I want this (pay, promotion, time off, etc.) and I didn't get it." Answering this question may help you discover the magnitude of the problem. In some cases it will become clear that each party has incompatible goals and a simple complaint exists. In other cases, this question may clarify that pseudocomplaint or emotionalism exists. For instance, each party may discover that the issue is not what was imagined. Employees may have assumed that they were being moved or given a task as a form of punishment when the supervisor considered it a way of rewarding them. There may also be other economic and environmental reasons that need to be considered.

"When does the problem need to be settled?" is the second question that should be answered. Time restrictions can be an asset as well as a liability. Both parties should mutually agree on the time frame for settling complaints. Setting a specific time gives both parties a clearly defined goal and establishes a sense of urgency. When a solution is developed, it also gives each party a feeling of accomplishment and helps establish an air of cooperation.

"What is needed to solve the problem?" is the third question that dichotomizes disputes into manageable parts. The best time to answer this question is when both parties are successful at solving the two previous questions (e.g., agreeing on a need and time to solve the problem). The climate should be pleasant and nonthreatening, with as few distractions as possible. The discussion between two parties will depend on the type of complaint. In some cases each may agree that additional information, in the form of facts and opinions, will be needed before a solution can be proposed. In a situation where each party wants responsibility or control over a program, each party will gather relevant information. This might include listing preliminary data about what type of information will be needed, where it can be obtained, or the cost/benefits and past experience data when it is relevant. In other situations each may want to clarify who is responsible for completing the task. In these cases it becomes a matter of finding the person responsible for assigning the task and obtaining a statement, preferably in writing, on the scope and extent of each person's responsibility in this matter.

Conversely, each party may clearly understand who has the authority or responsibility, but there may be a disagreement in interpreting an organizational policy. As such, each person will need to explain why he or she disagrees with the choice of the other person. No two complaints are exactly alike, and the information needed in each case will never be exactly the same. The important point is to identify what information is needed and from whom before trying to settle the disagreement. Ample time should be devoted to resolving this question since it is the most critical one. In many cases it will require repeated backtracking before each person feels he or she has enough information to clarify responsibilities, obligations, views, attitudes, and actions.

REACHING AGREEMENT

If both parties have agreed that they have enough information and clarification from supervisors and other influential people, often the last question can be answered. At this point, there may be no dispute since any misunderstanding or false information will have been eliminated. Assuming that unresolved differences remain, it will be necessary to ask the final question, "How will the complaint be settled?

If each party has a goal that is incompatible with the other, there are three primary ways of alleviating a complaint. Reaching a consensus should be your first priority. It involves using a problem-solving approach in which both parties are involved in joint deliberation. Consensus involves one-on-one interaction that provides mutually acceptable solutions. It usually results in the conciliation of two radically opposing viewpoints. This tends to produce an averaging effect that adds stability to decisions and is especially valuable in times of dramatic change since it allows for adjusting to changing directions. Consensus is fairly easy to obtain if both parties are flexible and have a willingness to adjust their original expectations.

If there are no areas of agreement, then each person must be willing to modify the decision until there is some overlap of what each is willing to accept. If one person wants a certain goal and the other person wants an opposite goal, each must find a mutually beneficial third goal.

If no agreement can be reached, another means will be needed to solve the complaint. Many personnel managers become involved in resolving complaints through mediation. Mediation occurs when two people cannot resolve a complaint and it is therefore necessary to bring a third party into the discussion for this specific purpose. A mediator's role is to help the two parties reach a mutually agreeable solution. As a mediator the personnel manager acts as a catalyst. He or she usually clarifies the issues and key parts of each issue. To facilitate cooperation, the personnel manager will prevent and inhibit destructive messages between each party. The mediator will also try to keep the discussion open by helping each person see the other's viewpoint and creatively seek alternative solutions.

A mediator is always a neutral third party and usually an equal in status to the two disagreeing parties. No attempt is made to coerce or force one party to accept a particular choice. The main attributes to being a good mediator are to be a good and highly respected facilitator. Good mediators seek understanding and participation, and they are divergent thinkers who have a tendency to see many solutions to almost any problem. In other words, mediators will monitor discussions and promote rationality and understanding between disagreeing parties. They should be especially adept at using the feedback tools discussed in the last part of this chapter.

Arbitration can be used as a means of last resort. Unlike mediation, where the discussion is still arrived at by mutual agreement, arbitration requires that a third party make the final decision. The arbitrator will decide who is right, or partially right, and who is wrong. Many times the arbitrator's decision is a compromise between two viewpoints, but it does not have to be a compromise wince the arbitrator controls the outcome.

An arbitrator's decision is final, and while it does provide solutions to conflicts it has many drawbacks. Instead of the discussion occurring between two parties, the focus now becomes one of persuading a third party. Very little meaningful communication occurs when the primary objective is to interrogate the second party and manipulate the arbitrator. Interrogation occurs when one reasons, "You know I am right, you are not admitting I am right, therefore it is up to me to get it out of you." While one may reason this way, there will be little progress since it is the other person who has control and can choose when to and when not to give honest answers.

Manipulative reasoning is, "It's up to me to get you unwittingly or unknowingly to say or do what I want you to." Each of the two parties will try to manipulate or sell the arbitrator on a recommended course of action. For the arbitrator to be effective, he or she must limit these tendencies if long-term solutions are to become a reality.

FEEDBACK TOOLS FOR MANAGING COMPLAINTS

To successfully manage complaints, you must become proficient at using the following feedback tools. Each of these tools can be learned and, with repeated practice, one can develop a skill in settling disagreements and clearing up misunderstandings.

To help answer each one of the four previous problem-solving questions (i.e., What is the complaint about?, When does the complaint need to be settled?, What is needed to solve the problem?, and How will the complaint be settled?), you should seek to first clarify areas of agreement and disagreement. To reach an agreement, neither party should lose sight of what has been accomplished and should keep the areas of disagreement in focus. In most discussions, people are usually surprised when they discover how much they agree with the other party and the common ground they share. By recording each point of agreement as it is achieved, the parties can become accustomed to successful problem solving. Each point that is successfully agreed upon makes the next consensus a little easier to reach. It is important to establish a sense of accomplishment, and this is most likely to occur when each party is reminded of past successful interaction. One way of increasing the effectiveness of this tool is to focus on areas of agreement, not disagreement. This limited focus not only keeps the disagreement in perspective, it also helps the discussion to remain positively oriented.

The usefulness of this tool is improved if each disagreeing person uses it. The personnel manager not only describes areas of agreement and disagreement, but also encourages the other individuals to describe areas of agreement and disagreement. Mutual use of this tool greatly improves its accuracy because at least twice the amount of feedback occurs. Each is also positively reinforcing the steps that need to be taken to settle the dispute.

Paraphrasing, which involves restating what was said by someone else, can also be used to manage complaints. To insure mutual understanding, paraphrasing should be used frequently by both parties. You should first listen to a key point or statement and then restate that point. Typically a paraphrased statement would start out as, "As I understand it, you're saying . . ." or "Let me be sure I am understanding you," or even "What you're saying is . . . ." Not surprisingly, the other person being paraphrased will reply, "No, I didn't mean (say) that!" It is not uncommon for the person to be surprised at his or her failure to make a point understood. Likewise, the paraphraser is often surprised at not being able to grasp the point being made. It is exactly these unchallenged and assumed meanings that cause disputes and prevent them from being settled. Paraphrasing is a simple tool that will make people become better listeners and become more involved in settling disputes.

Summarizing is another problem-solving tool. It involves frequently summing up the present direction of discussions and the accomplishments that have been achieved during the discussion. This tool helps focus the discussion, verify understanding of opinions expressed, improve communication, and assess progress toward some agreement. These occasional pauses in the conversation also give the parties time to collect their thoughts and reaffirm the direction and intent of the discussion. Like the other tools, it places the emphasis on positive accomplishments and de-emphasizes the negative aspects.

The last tool is called reverse roleplaying. It consists of each person assuming the role of his or her counterpart. Although it could be used in a one-on-one consensus-type approach, it would more likely be used by a mediator as a way of helping each understand the other's viewpoint. Some of these techniques are also applied to the situations described in chapter 8.

The environment and attitude of the personnel manager are important ingredients in resolving disagreements. In this chapter you were shown specific tools for establishing a healthy climate for solving complaints. Several tools dealing with attitudes were also reviewed that can enhance your ability to solve conflicts. Beyond these points, advice was given on how to manage, regardless of the climate or attitude. The following are the specific tools you can use to resolve disputes:

- listen more, talk less
- delay discussion (if necessary)
- clarify solutions
- develop consensus
- arbitration
- clarify areas of agreement and disagreement
- paraphrasing
- summarizing

4

Interviewing Complaining Personnel

This chapter is concerned with the informal daily interview that is part of every personnel manager's responsibilities. Interview here is defined as those one-on-one conversations between you and someone else. For you these conversations can also be preventative in nature by your seeking to discover potential misunderstandings and eliminate them. They can also serve a retroactive function when they are used to clarify misunderstandings and obtain an accurate picture of others' thoughts and attitudes. Finally, they can be used to help you grasp an understanding of various procedures, methods of operation, or other specialized knowledge.

Being able to communicate one-on-one with employees and others about a complaint is one of the most difficult and important aspects of being an effective personnel manager. It is needed when counseling employees who have emotional, personal, or drug problems or when simply discussing employee grievances. The benefits are obvious when handling those grievances and can be an important tool for maintaining harmony and productivity in the organization.

Interviews are used because you want to make sure your employees clearly understand how you think they are doing. Second, you want to eliminate any misunderstanding, which involves straightforward and honest discussions with ample questions and answers. Next you should plan on establishing a program designed to improve the situation and employees' performance. Last, the objective of interviews should be to build confidence between you and your personnel. Your own objectives should be to inform, encourage, and give recognition.

Interviews can be used whenever managers need to learn why some particular person is having difficulty completing a project or when they need to know the reason why an objective is not being reached. Interviews are also used to discover why some people are making costly and time-consuming mistakes even though the directions appear quite clear. In each one of the above situations, the reasons may range from a basic lack of interest in a project to a general resentment of managers and whatever they try to accomplish. They can be used to problem solve by

1. defining the problem,
2. generating possible solutions,
3. evaluating those solutions,
4. deciding what solution is best,
5. determining how to implement the solution, and
6. assessing how the solution solved the problem.

Finally, this process can simply be used to obtain information by those who want to be current.

To accomplish these objectives you must plan. Review what you will say and have specific good and bad points that should be noted. Anticipate what employee reactions might be to your comments. Have constructive measures available but give honest opinions. You can start with small talk, but quickly focus on the matter at hand—both of you know why you are there. The following checklist presents actions you should plan to take.

PLANNING CHECKLIST

1. Did you find a setting for the interview in a quiet, comfortable, and relaxed place?
2. Did you refresh your memory by reviewing the employee's job description, performance standards, job objectives, employee education, training, and experience?
3. Did you give your employee enough advance warning of the interview?
4. Did you ask your employee to come to the interview prepared to appraise his or her own performance?

*5. In your advance warning, did you make it clear that the purpose of the interview was to resolve the problem?

6. Do you know why the employee's performance is not up to standards?
7. Make sure you understand what the reasons are for the difference between what was expected and what was achieved.
8. Have an idea of what can be done to help the employee meet necessary goals.

*9. Did you note what reaction you think the employee will have and how you plan to handle this reaction?

*10. Do you keep a detailed list of facts supporting your recommendation?

*11. Have you made a list of corrective actions you plan to take?

*12. Have you written down any approach you plan to use to help gain the employee's acceptance of your corrective action?

*13. Have you noted what follow-up activities you can use?

The items indicated by * in this checklist presuppose a very directive form of counselling. A nondirective approach, in which the counselor tries to guide the employees to see the problem more clearly and attempt to arrive at their own solution, is discussed through examples in the latter part of the chapter.

There are specific techniques that can be used to make these one-on-one interviews more productive. In almost all complaint situations there are questions to be asked and there is the act of listening to the response of complainers. Communicating at a high level means becoming adept at both functions.

ASKING THE RIGHT QUESTIONS

No matter what is used to initiate conversation at the beginning of the meeting you must clearly state the purpose of the conversation. It is disastrous when someone feels betrayed or misunderstands the intention of the interviewer. Enormous damage has been done when someone believes that, "I had no idea why he was asking me those questions. If I had known, I wouldn't have said anything."

Since the purpose of a discussion is not always clear and because people do not always listen attentively, it is usually wise to occasionally re-emphasize or restate the purpose of the conversation before beginning detailed discussions. A good lead-in statement might be, "As I said, I would like to know . . . because I am planning to . . . ." This is only one example of a possible lead-in phrase that restates the purpose. You need to develop a phrase with which you are comfortable and one that is sincere. Regardless of the purpose statement, managers will want to tell the other person specifically how he or she can accomplish the overall objective of the interview. Again, such simple statements might include, "O.K., I would like you to tell me what you believe the problem is with . . ." or "I would like to know what you think about . . . ."

Telling someone what is needed should be the purpose of the transition statement that leads into the body, or main section, of the conversation. The body is where you will accomplish your intended objectives. It is at this point that specific questions are asked that provide the manager with needed information. Typical questions used in the body of an interview include, "How do you feel about . . ." or "Where did you actually notice . . . ." Each series of questions will be based on the type of information needed. In some cases you may want to understand someone else's feelings or thoughts about a specific event or project.

Whenever you want to understand the depth of someone's feelings or thoughts, you can use a funnel approach. This approach involves using a determined series of questions that seek to focus on a specific attitude, feeling, or perception. Such a series starts with very broad questions and progresses toward more focused questions that require more detailed answers. Through this process, a person can draw out the person being questioned and determine the degree of acceptance, commitment, disagreement, resentment, or resistance to your proposal. A funnel series of questions is illustrated below.

1. "What do you think is the attitude of others toward this . . . ?"
2. "What do you think of this situation?"
3. "What do you think about being assigned those duties for this project?"
4. "How do you feel about being given the task of completing it by the first of the month?"
5. "How are you going to complete the task by that date?"
6. "What special information do you need before you can complete it?"

As can be seen, there is a gradual focusing of the questions. Questions 1 and 2 are rather general in nature and give you time to evaluate the general acceptance of the project. Questions 3 and 4 are more immediate in nature because these questions seek to clarify someone else's specific feelings and commitment to the project. The last two very specific and detailed questions seek to isolate any ambiguous thoughts and clarify for both people exactly what will be needed before the task is completed. Obviously, the questions in any conversation will vary depending on the situation. However, the same pattern of general-to-specific questions is more likely to produce greater understanding.

The funnel approach is not the only possible structure. An opposite approach, referred to as a cone or narrow-to-broad approach, might be useful. For example, this approach could be used if you want better to understand a person's attitudes or thoughts. Instead of focusing on specific attitudes, you might be interested in exploring a person's reactions to a wide range of possible actions. A typical cone sequence would be similar to the following questions asked to a first-line supervisor by a personnel manager:

1. "How are you planning to handle these complaints?"
2. "What do you think about the way these complaints will be handled?"
3. "How can our department help you?"

The sequence begins with detailed questions and progresses toward broader questions about the value of a manager's functions. It allows you to develop a general understanding and acquire a greater range of information about what is needed to increase your value and that of your department. Questioning supervisors may help them clarify their values as well. Of course, at any point the manager may decide to reverse the structure and focus on some particular remark made by the supervisor.

The funnel and cone approaches are designed to draw out specific information about particular areas of concern; however, there are times when it is necessary for the personnel manager to leave the information being received unstructured. Sometimes it will be necessary to simply allow complaining individuals to explain their point of view. One technique for doing this is the open-ended question.

The value of open-ended questions as a technique for managing complaints is that each question encourages those who are complaining to provide desired information. Open-ended questions should be used in situations where a person is emotionally upset about someone else's action and wants to register a complaint.

This type of question not only helps you acquire information, it also helps the complaining person understand the topic under discussion. Open-ended questions help complainers freely choose the direction of the conversation. By so doing they will usually be more inclined to openly express themselves. Finally, open-ended questions can help complainers become actively involved in interviews and accept the responsibility for the content of the discussion. The following are only a few examples of open-ended questions:

1. "Why do you think they said that?"
2. "How are other things working out on the rest of the job?"
3. "Could you explain more about your responsibility in this area?"
4. "What was your understanding of the directive?"

In other words, open-ended questions are those that cannot be answered with a yes or no answer.

ACTIVE LISTENING

You will need to know how to listen as well as how to ask questions if the conversation is to provide useful information and be an effective management tool. Listening is the single most important element of the interview process. A willingness to listen is more than simply not talking. Not talking implies a passive attitude. For the conversation to be productive, you must become actively involved in acquiring, decoding, and clarifying information supplied by someone else.

The term *active listening* is most often associated with Carl Rogers. His nondirective approach to therapy emphasized the importance of listening to people's concerns in order to better understand them and for them to better understand themselves. It has now been adapted by many managers as an effective tool for reducing misunderstanding and conflict. Rogers defined the process as active listening because the listener has very specific responsibilities. He or she does not passively absorb the words spoken; instead, the listener actively tries to grasp the facts and feelings expressed and by listening tries to help the speaker solve his or her problems.

Active listening will not only help the manager acquire and understand more information, it also helps speakers gain a better understanding of their problems, accept responsibility for themselves, and generally increase their cooperativeness. For a personnel manager to actively listen, he or she must try to become aware of any personal bias. Prejudging the value of someone's statements or evaluating statements based on your own point of view will distort the information. Instead of prejudging or evaluating, try to view listening as an opportunity to learn how others feel or perceive some situation, not as a time to prepare a defensive response to criticism. Although active listening is essentially an attitude and a commitment to considering others' feelings, there are several ways to convince others that you are interested and listening.

To actively listen you must listen with a minimum of emotion and avoid biasing the speaker's responses. Obviously, disgusted, suspicious, or distrustful remarks or nonverbal gestures will prevent open communication. Negative remarks or gestures demonstrate that you are not really listening, but instead are evaluating the statements made. These evaluative remarks or gestures can easily provoke defensive responses in others, which prevent them from expressing their true emotions or attitudes.

While it may be obvious that you should not express negative attitudes, it is just as important to avoid expressing overtly positive reactions. Positive reactions are defined as those words and other gestures that can be seen as obviously enthusiastic. If a person sees that his or her comments elicit a positive response, he or she may bias further remarks. Nourishing expressions, as well as critical ones, alter the purpose of the interview, which is to obtain an accurate understanding of someone else's knowledge, feelings, attitudes, or perceptions. Because displaying your feelings is likely to influence someone else's comments, you will not receive reliable information. Often employees will slant the discussion to include comments that gratify and charm the manager instead of explaining their true thoughts and feelings. Half truths and elaborations can easily occur when someone is trying to impress and delight you with his or her competence, knowledge, or grasp of intricate and confusing matters.

Since employees usually need to be recognized and appreciated, they may succumb to the irresistible urge to make statements with which others will agree or reward in the form of smiles and other social reinforcement. A person might make a statement even though he or she does not believe it. Likewise, employees will avoid making disagreeable statements when they are positively reinforced to talk about "pleasant" topics. For one-on-one interviews to work effectively, the personnel manager must accept and even seek out the "bad" news as well as the "good" news from others.

It will be sufficient if you simply listen without overtly agreeing or disagreeing with the speaker. When people are supplied with unbiased, open-ended questions and an unemotional and impartial audience, they will more easily and openly express themselves in an unbiased manner.

Another technique that encourages an employee to talk but does not slant the information is the use of neutral utterances and gestures. These are nonword sounds and phrases or gestures that encourage the employee to keep talking but do not judge the worth of his or her statements. Such utterances would include sounds like "uh-hum" or "humm." When one of these sounds is made after an employee has spoken, it prompts him or her to expand upon the original statement.

Nonverbal gestures can also be used to encourage the employee to speak further, for example head nodding. A couple of subtle nods at the end of someone's statements imply that you have understood the comments and wish for the person to continue the conversation. If you combine nods with direct eye contact, others will feel more comfortable. For many, crossing one's arms in front of one's chest can be seen as overly judgmental so this should be avoided whenever possible. In general, taking a relaxed stance or leaning slightly forward when sitting are other ways of helping someone disclose his or her attitudes or knowledge. Therefore, to be a good listener you must be aware of your own nonverbal gestures and understand how they might be perceived.

One other technique often used to show concern is paraphrasing. As already noted, paraphrasing, or repeating someone else's statements in your own words, can be used to obtain information as well as settle complaints. In a normal informative conversation, it is wise to occasionally restate what the speaker has said. Statements like, "As I understand it, you're saying . . ." or "So you believe that . . ." are common paraphrased comments. This tool not only is an effective listening technique, it also helps clarify the normal misunderstandings that may arise during a conversation.

A PROBLEM SITUATION

The following illustrations help demonstrate interviews that can be used both to gather information and to resolve problems between people. While only limited aspects of communication can be demonstrated here, you should remember the main components of all conversations. If the managers are to effectively use interviews, they must ask open-ended questions, listen actively, and be encouraging in a neutral manner.

Obtaining Information

This first illustration demonstrates how to go about obtaining information from personnel within the organization. For example, suppose that a first-line supervisor is resisting attempts to implement a new program within his area. Since you, the personnel manager, are directly in charge of the program, you will need the assistance and support of the supervisor and employees if the plan is to be successful. As in any conversation, it should be considered within the context of your relationship with the individuals involved. Some relationships will generate more formal or less formal discussions, but the following is a representative sample of the responses that a manager could make to the supervisor. If the supervisor makes the following statement to you, what would you do?

> *Supervisor*: (speaking to you) "Look, this thing is never going to work for my department. It's going to make my men really confused and I don't see why we need it!"

At this point you can reply in several ways. You must choose the most effective response if the interview with the supervisor is to provide useful information. You could say:

1. "The proposal was approved by management, you'll just have to go along with it!"
2. "This is the first I've heard of this; don't you understand what you're supposed to do?"
3. "O.K., Allen (supervisor), just relax. So what seems to be the problem?"
4. "Don't get upset. You'll understand how it works after it has been in effect for awhile."
5. "I appreciate your concern. Now, why do you think it won't work?"

Obviously, many other responses could have been made, but these should illustrate the effective and ineffective approaches. In reviewing each of the possible replies, ask yourself what feeling would probably be generated by each of the statements. Are there any that show a negative or unconcerned attitude? Are there any that might initiate communication between the two people?

The first statement ("The proposal was approved by management . . .") would be very critical even if it were softened. It shows a disregard for others because you essentially tell the supervisor to unquestioningly carry out the project and that you do not intend to help the supervisor understand the situation. This is the type of response that most people would see as harmful, but it is nevertheless one of the more common ways of responding to the situation.

The second statement ("This is the first I've heard of this; don't you understand . . .") implies that you are uninformed about the project and the people involved in it. It confirms the supervisor's suspicion about the personnel manager's naïveté and also distorts what the supervisor said. The supervisor did not say that he did not understand, only that there was a problem. The supervisor would probably react to this statement in a defensive manner and might even accuse you of intentionally distorting what was said. Such responses on your part will usually produce the need for defensive reactions and means the conversation will have to be started over, if in fact you are still on speaking terms with each other.

The third reply ("O.K., Allen, just relax. So what seems to be the problem?") is better than the two previous ones, but it still is not the best approach. The first part of the statement projects a warm and concerned attitude, but you end by asking "What's the problem?" It implies that you have not heard what was said. It is the kind of remark that is not particularly destructive, just rather thoughtless.

The fourth possible statement ("Don't get upset. You'll understand how . . .") again shows some concern for someone's feelings, but then closes with vague and directionless advice. Essentially you are saying to forget about the problem, that in time it will solve itself. Because of this comment, several potential negative reactions could occur, the least of what is that the listener would view you as incompetent. It is doubtful that you would receive any future support or recognition from him.

The last comment ("I appreciate your concern. Now why do you think it won't work?") again begins with a warm and concerned attitude but adds an additional positive ingredient. It is the most open-ended and unbiased of the five possible responses. The person has already indicated that a problem exists. It is up to you to discover the details of the problem. Since anyone will find it difficult to be current with all the details of a project, the comment has an additional advantage. It allows you time to collect your thoughts and understand the line of reasoning used by the supervisor. The fifth response gives him the opportunity to explain the rationale for his previous statement and show that you are ready to listen. It is clearly the most productive choice.

Although one remark will not always show someone else that you are listening, interested, and sincerely want to help solve the problem, this last remark will certainly begin to build this attitude. Consistently adopting this willingness to listen approach to similar situations will not only help you collect accurate and truthful information, but also help solve problems that arise as in the following situation.

Interviews as Problem Solvers

Kay Myers is a personnel manager who has just been approached by a subordinate and hears the following comments: "Kay, you have got to do something with the printing and duplication office. Every time I try to have the training manual sent over there, the printing and duplicating supervisor hassles me and says she will get to it when she can. If she doesn't go on and do her job, I can't be responsible when the job falls behind schedule."

Now Kay has a problem. Often her first reaction might be to respond based on what she knows about the printing supervisor. As Kay, first of all, assume that the subordinate is a friend of yours and the key link in accomplishing the task. On the other hand, the printing supervisor is not one of your favorite people. She always seems to be complaining, and in fact many call her "old grouch." Placed squarely between the two people, it seems to imply favoring one side or the other.

Assuming that you are concerned about how your subordinate feels, you can ask for details about the trouble (using open-ended questions). Through this process your subordinate explains that the printing supervisor refused to accept some of the material and told him to fill out some forms and she would deal with it when she could. The printing supervisor even told him that if he had done his job there would be no rush to do the job. Add to this information the knowledge that your subordinate has told others about the trouble (so several people will be waiting to see what will be done), and you have a problem.

Unlike the previous situation in which the conversation occurred on the spur of the moment, this time you have the opportunity to plan what will be done. Assume that you have had some contact with the printing supervisor in the past and therefore have a preconceived attitude toward her. Obviously, you need to be aware of any bias that you have because these preconceived ideas can adversely affect the conversation. If you do not recognize your own bias, the following unproductive attitudes might be communicated:

1. Your subordinate is more important to the task than the printing supervisor.
2. There would be no trouble if "old grouch" had done what she was supposed to do.
3. Everyone is watching me. I have to stand up for myself—I'll show her who's in charge!
4. That printing supervisor had better do this job or I'll have to talk to her boss.

These destructive attitudes will adversely affect future contacts with her. If the communication is to be successful, there is no place for personal viewpoints or preferences.

In addition to avoiding negative reactions, you also need to be aware of possible negative reactions from the printing supervisor. She might resent you or feel you have no power over her and therefore have no right to discipline her. She may even try to show how she was right and your subordinate wrong.

Although there are at least a thousand variations that the interview could take, the soundness of your decisions will be improved if the following approach is used.

Start the conversation by identifying the existing problem. The printing supervisor should not be under the false belief that this is merely a social call or be surprised by the purpose of the conversation.

State the problem, using an open-ended question rather than a biased one. Biased questions would be: "What is the matter with you?" or "Is there some reason why you can't do the work?" Productive and unbiased open-ended questions include: "What's going on between you and my subordinate?" or "How did this argument come about?"

Use active listening to help clarify and resolve the problem. Much will depend on how much the printing supervisor trusts you and how well she is able to verbally communicate with you. However, at the very least it will show that you value her contribution to the project and that you recognize her worth.

Always explore the parameters of the problem. Discover what situational factors are helping create the problem. To achieve this objective you must avoid placing blame on the printing supervisor. Statements like "Do you like what you do!" or "Don't you like my subordinate!" display a preconceived and negative attitude toward the supervisor. Better questions that explore the parameters are "How do you feel about having to complete this by the first of the month?" or "How do you feel we should go about completing the printing by the first of the month?"

Involve the other person in resolving the problem. The purpose of this interview is to obtain information that satisfies some need. In this case the information can be used to eliminate the problem. From information supplied by the supervisor it may become evident that the work needs to be reorganized, or that there is a personality clash between the two employees or that some other factor is the primary cause of the incident. The person supplying the information will usually have very useful comments or ideas, if the climate promotes open communication.

Frank discussion can help the supervisor see the incident within a larger framework and have less need to see the situation as a win/lose battle between himself and Kay or her subordinate. As the printing supervisor openly interacts, she is likely to see the situation as larger than her disagreement with the other person and not likely to feel her ego is still being challenged. In any case, the supervisor is the one most likely to have the solutions and communication skills and honest answers that will help you develop the most reasonable solutions.

This situation is not necessarily critical, but it does give Kay a chance to practice interpersonal skills. With enough practice at one-on-one communication, we can all learn how to handle a variety of situations in which information is needed to solve problems or acquire a better understanding of some situation.

As to solving a problem, you are not obligated to take someone's advice, but the interview process is a tool that provides flexibility in dealing with people and helps to clarify what others are thinking or feeling.

Interviewing skills simply make a manager better able to deal with other people because they allow the manager to become more effective at the interpersonal relationships that are part of every job. It also makes the overall climate of the organization more agreeable. The listening techniques and open-ended questions of the interview process are valuable tools. When employees and fellow managers believe that you are fair and easy to talk to, they will learn to accept and trust your actions. In turn, when employees feel this way about themselves, it makes accomplishing individual and departmental objectives much easier.

Better listening by the manager to employee concerns promotes better listening and cooperation among employees. You can increase the probability of good communication if you ask yourself several questions.

- Did you give your personnel ample time to raise questions or make comments?
- Were you objective?
- Did you evaluate their situation, not their personality?
- Did you have them evaluate their own performance?
- Do your employees understand their job and responsibilities?

- Did they leave with specific plans on how to improve and what's expected of them?

5

Peer Review

Up to this point we have only examined the one-on-one process for resolving complaints. Traditionally, employee complaints are resolved by the supervisor, human resource manager, or upper-level manager directly interacting with the employee. This interaction varies from the one-on-one confrontation to "open-door" policies. In each of the bases the assumption and practice revolve around a manager's or managers' directly resolving an employee's complaint.

These one-on-one management reviews of employee complaints usually put the problem-solving responsibility and power squarely on the shoulders of either the supervisor or human resource manager. Obviously, this can cause a problem when complaints revolve around the relationship between the supervisor and the employee. Even if there is no problem between the complaining employee and the supervisor or human resource manager, other difficulties can occur.

Many employees will see the grievance and employee complaint process as nothing more than a rubber stamp process. Right or wrong, many will believe that once a supervisor or human resource manager makes a decision, others above that manager will be extremely reluctant to override those lower-level decisions. Whether or not this assumption is true, such an attitude can lead to distrust of the system. It can also result in employees not using the process. As a result, only the most severe cases of dissatisfaction surface—those involving discipline and discharge. Meanwhile, other more subtle conditions affecting employment and productivity remain hidden. Once less restrictive and intimidating conditions are removed, those more subtle factors affecting performance, like disagreement over merit evaluation, promotion disappointment, and so forth, can be evaluated. In the end, the complaint process can result in better employee understanding, a higher degree of peer acceptance, and better working relations, all of which result in greater satisfaction and better performance.

Peer review provides an effective alternative to the so-called open-door policy. Problems can occur even when a company boasts of offering employees an open-door policy. In most open-door policy situations, employees theoretically have open access to any management level. While this policy may be admirable in theory, in reality it is often different. Despite sincere good intentions, many employees may believe that they will not get a fair hearing. Others are hesitant about approaching management, with the natural status barriers that exist between employees and management. Few of us feel comfortable talking to our "superiors." Others will not use the open door policy simply because they fear it might hurt their careers or be degrading.

While traditional systems can be efficient, they are often ineffective, and when these systems are ineffectual, many employees may choose to leave the company. Some will also seek satisfaction outside the company in the form of third-party intervention (e.g., legal systems, equal opportunity employment commission, union, etc.).

EMPLOYEE INVOLVEMENT

Peer review and resolution of employee complaints are effective alternatives to traditional one-on-one and open-door complaint systems. Using this process is a tangible way for management to demonstrate its commitment to and support of greater employee involvement.

Frequently, upper managers claim that they want greater employee participation. Often they talk of sharing the decision making, but in reality it is only talk. There is no evidence, no action that indicates top management is sincere about great employee involvement.

It is easy to understand employee cynicism. Publicly employees hear top management talk of trust, openness, employee involvement, and the importance of front-line personnel, while in private it is business as usual. There is no sharing of power, no treatment of individuals as adults. Instead, department and status lines are drawn and authoritarian culture remains. Most employees are treated as if only a few have the desire and intelligence to make important decisions.

Proper management of complaints requires that employees be brought into the decision-making process. Peer review is a powerful means of attaining active employee participation and in turn more effective decision making.

When peer review systems are used instead of one-on-one management reviews, the process can be perceived almost immediately as more fair and less intimidating. After all, you are being evaluated by your peers; what could be more fair? Of course, simply seeing the benefits of such a system is not enough to insure it will be a successful tool. A great deal of thought must go into ensuring it is properly designed. For instance, employees chosen to review employee complaints must have the training and decision-making tools to do a good job. Good peer review systems do not happen by accident. As we shall see, it takes a coordinated effort.

Once an organization has installed a well-coordinated peer review system, it is generally perceived to be more fair and less intimidating than traditional systems. This being the case, there is a high probability that there will be more complaints, not fewer. However, this is not bad; it is decidedly good. It is better to resolve complaints early than to let them grow and infect the whole organization. Remember, unresolved complaints can cause some employees to quit the job and leave and others just to quit trying and stay. The end result is lower productivity and cooperation.

Employee attitudes and perceptions are more likely to be positive when they see positive changes occurring. With peer review, management not only says that it wants shared decision making, it demonstrates it. Companies that have used the peer review system report that after only one or two hearings, employees begin to realize that the process works. They also realize that they have gained a vehicle for their decision-making power.

Many companies implementing a peer review system report that within a few months there is a noticeable improvement in employee relations. Clearly employees have evidence of management's commitment and, in turn, management sees that employees do make good decisions. Despite fears about the effectiveness of peer review, organizations who have used it, like General Electric, express great support for the program (Boisseau, 1983; Finney, 1988). Employees do not (as is sometimes feared) side with fellow employees (Mauer, 1986). In fact, many say that peer review committees tend to be stricter with fellow employees than management might.

Another potential advantage of peer review is consistency. Supervisory application of policies and procedures can be enhanced through peer review. Since there is no longer a perfunctory process, supervisory personnel must improve their ability to accurately and consistently apply company policies and procedures. It reduces inconsistencies between departments because everyone is more or less involved in resolving problems and understanding the problem-solving process. Finally, peer review tends to create less third-party intervention. This occurs primarily because of employees' greater faith in the internal problem-solving process.

TYPES OF PEER REVIEW SYSTEMS

There is no universal or standard form of peer review system. Procedures and systems for peer reviews vary greatly from one organization to another. These committees go by various names, including employee problem-solving groups, appeals boards, and so forth. They not only vary in name, they also vary in size and makeup.

Sometimes these peer groups only include employees; however, this is an extremely rare situation. More commonly, they consist of both management and employees. The number of members in each group varies from organization to organization. Many contain five or six members, with some recommending an odd number so tie votes do not occur.

Let us assume that the peer group consists of six members. In this situation we might expect three of them to be employee members. Usually a complaining employee will then randomly select those three members to hear his/her case. In some cases, members of the peer review committee are drawn from a pool of potential reviewers. Managers will then select three members who will sit in the session. In other cases, it is the complaining employee who both randomly draws several names from a pool of potential employee members and then chooses a limited number from that group to hear the complaint.

The management side of the review committee is often composed of various middle managers, usually including the human resource director. There are two primary reasons for having the human resource director be a permanent member of the committee: he or she is most likely to have in-depth and accurate knowledge of company policies and procedures, and he or she can also be a valuable source of information that might be relevant to the case. Generally speaking, these directors are the best managers to participate in peer review.

QUALIFICATIONS

When forming a peer review group, one should pay special attention to the qualifications members need. Managers should ask, "What manager is qualified to make a judgment in this case?" Special attention should be given to potential conflicts of interest. If a management member has a potential conflict of interest, then a substitute should be found. This would be the case when a manager is scheduled to hear the complaint of one of his or her subordinates.

Qualifications of employees often revolve around their knowledge. In order to make a decision concerning the complaint, employees must have knowledge of policies and procedures. Many companies deal with the problem of employee qualification through a combination of experience and training. For instance, a rule might be that only employees who have been with the company for five years or more and who have completed specific training would be able to hear the case. This training would be designed to familiarize employees with the corporate, legal, and ethical considerations needed to render a decision. Unfortunately, sometimes hourly employees have been requested to attend review sessions with as little as a thirty-minute warning.

DECISIONS

While employee members may vary greatly in their preparation and training, one area that tends not to vary from one organization to another is the decision-making domain of the committee. Frequently, when decisions will significantly affect corporate finances, the decision is passed to upper management. Discrimination cases are also generally treated separately. In discrimination cases, the complaining individual can usually appeal even the review committee's decision (which is normally final) to the company's director of affirmative action.

Discrimination and other purely legal matters demand special attention, as discussed in chapters 6 and 7. From a legal standpoint, the review committee should never conflict with court cases involving some complaint. Whether implied or explicit, organizations usually have a rule against any review committee passing judgment on cases that have already been taken outside the company. You can easily see the problem if the judgment of the inside review committee conflicts with the judgment of an outside court system.

Usually peer review decisions (beyond those involving discrimination or legal matters) are final, but in some cases employees can appeal a decision. An employee would first take a complaint to the immediate supervisor. If that employee were unhappy with that decision, it could be appealed to the review committee. Then the judgment of the peer review committee would become final. However, it must be emphasized that no particular approach is universally used. Occasionally the peer review process is the middle stage, with front-line supervisors being the first stage and upper management the last stage.

Most organizations limit the amount of time that an employee has to file a complaint. These time restrictions are usually quite liberal, but this in itself can pose a problem. If complaints are not handled quickly, the effectiveness of the decision is impaired. As soon as possible (ASAP) is an invitation for misuse or lack of use. The ideal situation is to establish strict time standards within which each complaint must be given full attention. An example of such a standard might read, "Decisions on employee appeals should be made within ten working days."

In some cases decisions of the committee are confidential, but most recognize the benefits of publicizing rulings that involve policies and procedures. The hope is that by publicizing such decisions, the company will avoid similar complaints because others can learn from the ruling. Remember, review committees can only interpret applications of policies and procedures; they cannot change the rules. Sometimes the committee will see a change that needs to be made and it will make a recommendation. The committee itself cannot make policy changes. This function remains the exclusive responsibility of upper management.

GENERAL ELECTRIC—A CASE STUDY

General Electric's Appliance Park-East facility in Columbia, Maryland, has had a great deal of success implementing its own form of peer review. In this facility a five-member review committee composed of three employees and two management members is used. As a result of this distribution, the control, technically speaking, rests with employees who have the majority vote. Despite some concerns for turning over the ultimate power to employees, it worked quite well. Not only has this system been very successful, but it has also enhanced the cooperation, trust, and employee relations within the organization (Boisseau 1983, 76–79). This positive environment was not always the case at the G. E. facility.

In the 1970s this G. E. facility was the target of unionization attempts, which included six separate representation elections. Although unionization attempts were unsuccessful, G. E.'s winning majorities were constantly under 60 percent (Boisseau 1983, 76–79). These elections proved to be detrimental to the organization for they divided opinions and decreased morale.

To G. E.'s credit, in the early 1980s management started changing its relationship with the employees. Managers knew that improving the grievance process was one of the key ways of both enhancing human relations and, at the same time, helping reduce the desire to unionize.

G. E. examined the grievance situation and discovered a steady decline in the usage of the grievance process. Part of the decline was attributed to better supervision and more consistent application of policies (Boisseau 1983, 76–79). On the other hand, management knew that part of the decline was due to their employees' basic lack of faith in the grievance process.

Recognizing the problem with the grievance system, Joe Carando, then plant manager, recommended the establishment of an employee review system. Up to this point he had the final authority. Under the peer review system, managers decided that each of the five members would have one vote. Each vote counted equally. As already noted, the committee would consist of three employees and two management personnel. It was hoped that this distribution would prove management's commitment to improve relations. It was also decided that the committee decisions would be final and binding.

As you might imagine, there was some initial skepticism from both managers and employees; however, upper management believed that the process would prove its worth. Managers at G. E. wanted their employees to understand that they trusted them.

Before installing the review system, a great deal of groundwork had already occurred. Management had previously focused on helping employees understand what is needed to successfully run a business. Many of the employees had also taken a two-year self-development program that identified the major functions of their programs. Employees were encouraged to ask questions about why things were done the way they were. In these self-development classes, employees and managers also discussed how the new grievance procedure would work.

Before the peer review system was implemented, management scheduled an after work meeting to review the new system and hear recommendations on the proposed program. At that meeting, some recommendations were made and thirty-nine employees volunteered to participate in the necessary training. Each of them completed an eight-hour program that explained the legal and ethical elements of the grievance process. They were also exposed to some problem-solving and listening techniques. Then they began.

Implementation

In the actual review process, the complaining employee randomly draws the names of four potential panelists from a pool of sixty hourly employees. The complaining employee can choose to discard one name so that he or she has three employee representatives. These three then have the opportunity to withdraw if they choose. The committee also consists of two permanently assigned managers, including the human resource manager.

G. E. encourages complaining employees to first discuss the matter one-on-one with their supervisors. If that does not solve the problem, then they present their case to the peer review committee. Both sides then present their case before the committee. The committee can interview anyone it thinks may be relevant to the case. It also has access to the employee's files.

The committee then makes a decision. It may decide to modify the complaint as well as grant or issue a denial of the grievance. The vote on these issues is by secret ballot. When the judgment is announced, a statement is issued explaining the decision.

According to Jack Hoffman, an organizational and development specialist at G. E., the process at G. E. has worked extremely well (Finney 1988, 45). He noted a survey showing that 82 percent of the plant staff was satisfied with the peer review process. Of the 300 grievances filed at the facility in the last five years, only 100 went to the review panel. The others were resolved by the employees and their supervisors.

Hoffman also states that employees, because of the peer review, are more likely to accept the judgments of the committee than when those judgments came from management. He said that even when a dissatisfied employee goes to an outside agency like the Equal Employment Opportunity Commission (EEOC), G. E. feel confident. Hoffman said, when investigators see the peer approach they usually do not even go through the paperwork (Finney 1988, 45).

There is a great deal of variation in the way peer review processes operate. Sometimes complaining employees are paid when they appear before the committee; in other cases they are not. Sometimes the majority of the committee is made up of managers but, as the G. E. case shows, this is not always so.

Most of these review committees decide purely employee grievances, but sometimes they are used by managers to resolve grievances among their peers. Some of the peer reviews are run very formally, while others use a more informal style. Occasionally, employees must comply with management decisions before a ruling by the committee. In most cases employees are not bound until a ruling has been issued by the review committee.

Despite the variation, one fact is clear—they do work. They enhance the supervisor/employee relationship. They enhance the participative aspect of corporate culture much more so than do simple, but ineffective, open-door policies. They promote greater employee confidence in and commitment to the organization. They can enhance the culture because employees believe that they are being treated fairly and are trusted.

Peer review can demonstrate a real commitment by management but, like most tools, it must be properly administered. While each peer review system should be adapted to each organization, some common themes emerge. For instance, it is paramount that the company spend adequate time training both employees and managers in the use of the system. It is wise to get front-line supervision's involvement at the beginning of the implementation. These people are the ones who will be most directly affected and their input can be invaluable. Next, it is wise to effectively market the program to employees and managers so that volunteers can be secured. Finally, always plan on fine tuning. Make improvements and changes that will keep the program dynamic and responsive to the needs of the organization.

REFERENCES

Boisseau, R. T., and H. Caras. 1983. A radical experiment cuts deep into the attractiveness of unions. *Personnel Administrator* 28, no. 10 (October): 76–79.

Finney, M. I. 1988. A good idea—five years later. *Personnel Administrator* 33 (March): 45.

Mauer, G. W., and J. Flores. 1986. Peer review and employee advocacy in conflict resolution process. *Personnel Administrator* 31, no. 6 (June): 53–58.

Human Relations Learning Exercises

EXERCISE 1
NOBODY'S LISTENING

The purpose of this exercise is to show participants what it is like to feel the frustration of not being heard. This exercise should be used *before* going over the need to listen or any of the other learning activities described in the following pages. This exercise should be thought of as an attention-getting step that promotes the need to listen.

The exercise should take about thirty minutes to complete. Plan to have a flip chart or chalkboard to summarize key points.

Process:

1. You should tell participants about the objective of the activity. Next, break the group into pairs of participants and give each pair a copy of the role play. You can use the ones provided or make up your own based on your own experiences.
2. Each member of the pair chooses a role and studies it for about three minutes. Everyone should begin the exercise at the same time.
3. It is very important that you make sure each participant in each pair is *not* listening to the other. You should challenge those who are listening.
4. When you feel the group has reached the maximum frustra-

tion (usually occurs when noise level increases dramatically), then stop the activity and discuss how the participants felt and how they responded to the frustration.

Consider the following situation. Jan, a production supervisor, and Ralph, a warehouse assistant, are discussing the use of a new computer system that is currently being implemented. They and others are trying to develop a compatible system. Just before the meeting, Marsha, Ralph's close friend, told him, "Jan is such a squirrel. I've heard she'd like to use the new computer program to take over the inventory system." Jan has been told by her friends that Ralph is overbearing and never looks on the positive side. Each individual will assume either the role of Ralph or Jan. The meeting starts:

Ralph: You know, not everyone around here is going to go for this system they're trying to implement.

Jan: Yeah! It's going to be a pain, but we've got to do it.

Ralph: Well, I don't know about you, but I think we've got to have more time to debug the system before we can get it up and running.

Jan: I'm going to need my own computer terminal or else this whole discussion, from my point of view, is a waste of time.

Ralph: (interrupting Jan) Do you think you're the only one that needs the terminal!

Jan: As I mentioned before, I don't know about you, but my department has to have the third software package we reviewed.

Ralph: I think you're being petty about that. If you keep this up you're wasting my time.

EXERCISE 2
RESOLVING COMPLAINTS THROUGH COMMUNICATION

The purpose of this exercise is to held participants evaluate the negative as well as positive aspects of communication used to resolve employee complaints. The exercise should also help participants improve communication skills.

This exercise can be performed with any size group and takes approximately one and one-half hours to complete. Material needed to do the exercise includes the role play descriptions and the positive/negative evaluation forms described in the following pages.

Process:

1. You should first review the material in chapter 2 on creating an atmosphere for resolving complaints (or other supplemental material for resolving complaints) *before* the exercise begins. Specifically, you should be sure to emphasize the need for:

- practicing effective listening
- improving the accuracy of communication
- eliminating barriers to resolving complaints

For example, focus on constructive communication, de-emphasize the win/lose perspective, project a good attitude, and so forth.

2. You should begin the exercise by first dividing all participants into pairs. Plan on having participants role play the communication exercises listed in the following pages. A minimum of four role plays should be used since this allows each person in the pair an opportunity to practice both destructive and constructive communication. You should make a point to explain to participants that in the first two rounds one member of the pair will role play the higher authority while the other person role plays a more

subordinate role. In rounds three and four, role plays should be reversed.

3. The next step is to give participants one of the role play exercises. Instruct everyone how the exercise will be conducted (see step two), and then give the pairs a few minutes to look over their role playing situations.

4. You should start the process of role playing and allow about six to eight minutes for participants to do the first role play. After this is done, hand each participant a copy of the evaluation form. Each person uses these forms to grade the two role plays that have occurred. The right side of the form shows the more constructive, cooperative, and supportive way to communicate. If most of the numbers are on the left, it signifies a more destructive, competitive, controlling, and defensive way of communicating. Such behavior tends to lead to more dissatisfied interactions and more employee complaints.

5. For each round, have participants put a mark on the evaluation sheet. Mark the sheets for round one by making a "1" at the appropriate place. Successive rounds should be marked "2", "3", and "4." The more positive the exercise, the further the numbers will move to the right side of the sheet. For example, if round one was perceived as more negative than round two, the number one will be more to the left. Allow each participant a few minutes to record his or her impression of the round. After this is done, each pair should discuss and compare its impressions of the first two rounds. This should take approximately four or five minutes.

6. Once round one is completed, you can start round two and then go through the process described above, including filling out the evaluation form. As noted above, this time instead of marking a "1" beside each category on the evaluation form, participants should mark a "2" since the evaluation pertains to their impression in round two. Future rounds should be graded in a similar manner. (You should develop role plays that are appropriate for your situations.)

7. Once all rounds are completed, reassemble the entire group and review key concepts. At this point you can start the discussion by asking participants questions that relate to the material on which

you have lectured and the results of the exercise. Topics can include the need to practice listening, the barriers that exist to resolving complaints, and how these barriers can be overcome. This discussion can also revolve around ways to de-emphasize the win/lose attitude, how to project good attitudes, how to communicate in a nonthreatening manner, and how to use the feedback tools mentioned in chapter 3.

8. Other role plays more appropriate for your particular situation can be developed using the same basic components of these role plays. You can also reduce the time needed to do the activity by not role playing rounds three and four.

ROLE PLAY # 1

(One participant will play Kay and one will play Roberta.)

Kay Myers is a personnel manager who has just been approached by a subordinate and hears the following comments: "Kay, you have got to do something with the printing and duplication office. Everytime I try to have the training manual sent over there, she (printing and duplicating supervisor) hassles me and says she will get to it when she can. If she doesn't go on and do her job, I can't be responsible when the job falls behind schedule."

Now you have a problem. First of all, assume that the subordinate is a friend of yours and the key link in accomplishing the task. On the other hand, the printing supervisor is not one of your favorite people. She always seems to be complaining and many people call her an "old grouch."

Assuming that you are concerned about how your subordinate feels, you can ask for details about the trouble. Through this process your subordinate explains that the printing supervisor refused to accept some of the material and told him to fill out some forms and she would deal with it when she could. The printing supervisor even told him that if he had done his job, there would be no rush to do the job. Add to this information the knowledge that your subordinate has told others about the trouble (so several people will be waiting to see what will be done), and you have a problem.

Objective

Your goal is to make the other person agree with you. You should explain the rationale supporting your approach. Remember, you are determined that your way will be implemented.

As the printing and duplication supervisor, Roberta Thomason, you are responsible for all graphics and printing within the plant. It seems that everyone is always trying to put through last-minute orders. Over the years you have generally concluded that most of these rush orders are due to poor planning. You believe that rush orders happen because somebody waited until the last minute to do something. You pride yourself on your organization and commitment and wish others cared as much about doing a good job as you do.

Typical of the problems you have been having is Kay Myers's (personnel manager's) new subordinate. Recently he came into your office with a you'll-have-to-take-care-of-this-right-now-or-else! attitude. He thought he had the most important job there was. You told him he would have to get in line along with everyone else, that business was on a first-come-first-served basis, and that he would be processed when his turn came. When he was told this he erupted and stormed out of the office.

Objective

Your goal is to get the other person to agree with you. You should explain the rationale supporting your approach. Remember, you are determined that your way will be implemented.

ROLE PLAY # 2

(One participant will role play Karen, the other Ralph.)

A medium-sized hospital is located in a community with several larger hospitals. It has a clinical laboratory of modest size and can perform most of the tests needed in the hospital's daily activities. The administrator is under pressure to make the hospital financially competitive and at the same time more attractive to physicians.

The associate administrator, Ralph Woods, is second in command. He has recently decided that the attractiveness to local physicians could be enhanced if a new state-of-the-art computer system were installed in the laboratory. The hospital administrator has requested that the associate administrator along with the laboratory manager, Karen Watkins, make a recommendation to purchase or not to purchase.

Ralph Woods strongly favors the purchase. He believes it will improve the hospital's reputation and make it more attractive to local physicians.

Karen Watkins, the laboratory manager, does not believe that the system will improve the laboratory's effectiveness. In fact, she foresees many problems with installing the system. Duplication of hardware will be necessary, vendor training does not include nursing personnel, and she understands that an interface for the laboratory's chemistry analyzer will not be available for at least a year.

Ralph has arranged a meeting with Karen to discuss this situation. He had mentioned to Karen his desire to purchase the computer system, and he was extremely distressed to hear of her opposition. Because Karen is Ralph's subordinate, she will be restricted as to what she can do.

The meeting starts:

Karen: Ralph, I know that we need to enhance our image with physicians, but there are other considerations besides image.

Ralph: Karen, you aren't going to start that stuff about cost, are you? I've already heard you mention that! It's not coming out of your budget. You ought to be glad to get a computer system.

Karen: But it's no help if it's going to cost more than it's worth!

Ralph: (with a disgusted look) That's your opinion! You obviously don't understand the "big picture."

Objective

Your goals are to create a climate to explore differences between you and the other person. Encourage the other person to express his or her position and then try to search for solutions that accomplish both of your objectives.

ROLE PLAY # 3

(One participant will play Martin and one will play Barry.)

Sure Electronics has had relative peace between its 350 labor force and management personnel. The last strike happened over thirty years ago when the present union at the plant was formed. Recently, however, there has been almost no progress on negotiations between labor and management.

The company has made a final offer to the union that consists of a $.15 an hour wage increase plus improved dental coverage. The union leadership agreed to present the offer to the membership for a vote, but it indicated to management that it believed the offer was unfair.

When the offer was presented to the union membership, it was generally condemned. The union leadership assured its members that they could get more. When the vote was taken less than 20 percent of the employees voted to accept the offer. The union decided to go on strike.

To get a feeling for the environment between management and labor, we can look at the perspective of two individuals. Martin

Shane is the chief shop steward at Sure Electronics. Barry Wilson is the assistant manager at the plant. The two have privately agreed to informally discuss their problems.

Martin Shane's Perspective

As chief shop steward at Sure Electronics, Martin Shane was recently asked about what caused the strike after so many years of peaceful coexistence. He said, "Well, everything hasn't been exactly peaceful around here." He went on to say that many people are upset because management always seems to be changing policies or procedures. Managers always try to increase production, regardless of the cost. For example, they always seem to want employees to operate more and more machines, instead of operating one piece of equipment really well. It is too much for one person. "After all," he said, "you've only got two hands and two eyes. How can they expect you to keep track of four or five pieces of equipment?"

Martin believes much of the labor unrest is due to management's always bringing in new supervisors from outside who do not understand the business. "It is hard to tell from one moment to the next what they are going to emphasize. One moment they are talking about quality-first and the next they are pushing the numbers. Keep the machines running at all cost, that's what they really want. Many of these new supervisors do not even know a good part from a bad one."

It is clear that management does not trust its employees. In the past, supervisors were promoted from the line. Under the current management, all new supervisors are brought in from the outside. "Not that you would want to be a supervisor," Martin continued, "but it seems that they think of you as a piece of equipment. To get someone who thinks, they think they have to go to the outside."

The union wants at least twice what management is offering. "Even at that, it is nothing to brag about. Management sounds like they are breaking their backs. They tell us that Sure Electronics is paying more than other companies. Even if it is true, it is not important. We're not working for other companies, we're working for this one and they are making plenty of money. They are making money while you break your back. We deserve a bigger piece of the pie, especially if the pie is getting bigger."

"Most of the employees feel that management is making plenty of money even though the company does not open its books to any of the union leadership. If they were on the up and up they would open them. Even if they do not open their books, there are signs everywhere that they are making money. Ten trucks leave these docks every day while only a few years ago only three or four would leave the docks. That is over triple the business and management still wants to give us a stingy raise."

"It seems the company is spending money right and left on new equipment and adding additional space. Already they have installed twice as much equipment this year as they did last year. Yet they do not want to pay for the help they have."

"It is even the little things that cause problems around here," Martin explained. "For example, supervisors do not even let employees off in time to wash up before they go home. Either they ought to build a bigger washroom or they should let us off in enough time so we can get cleaned up in order to leave on time. They have a fit if you are a couple of minutes late for work, but they don't mind keeping you late, or not letting you off in time so you won't be late leaving. They are always talking, never listening."

Objective

Your goal is to get the other person to agree with you. You should explain the rationale supporting your approach. Remember, you are determined that your way will be implemented.

Barry Wilson's Perspective

Barry Wilson is part of the "new management" at Sure Electronics. When management adopted a more competitive philosophy, it meant making some changes in management procedures. When

Bob Johnson (past plant manager) controlled operations, he spent most of his time in the plant. He knew everyone on a first-name basis, as he was one of those old-time managers who had come up through the ranks, starting out as a machinist. He had a very relaxed, permissive style. The plant seemed to run itself. Bob was a "good ole boy" and everyone liked him, but some took advantage of him.

When the company was bought out, Bob retired. "The old way of doing business is simply not possible today," Barry explained. "Times are tougher. The competition is eating our lunch. The Japanese, Germans and others are getting lean and mean, and we had to do the same or lose out. We are going down the tubes unless we make some changes. Wages are part of the changes. Offshore and Asian companies' labor costs are one-eighth or less of our costs. Lower wages are an essential part of our restructuring to make the corporation more competitive."

"Implementing new technology, updating some of the outdated equipment, and generally getting more 'bang for your bucks' is necessary in today's competitive world. Production and quality must become a process of continuous improvement."

"The current strike is in large part due to labor to show management that they don't like all these changes. Nevertheless, change is essential if our company is going to survive. You want to be fair, give good wages for a fair day's work, but that has to mean everyone adopting a more competitive posture."

"In the past, Sure Electronics had offered supervisory jobs to employees in the plant. This was the way it was done; however, it is now important that new blood be brought into the business if changes are going to be rapidly implemented. We need new ways of doing things, not just doing old things better. New perspectives are difficult with the current employees who are rather stuck in their ways. Besides, it is always difficult to go from employee to supervisor. Not many can divorce themselves from their former friends and become the boss. It is a whole different way of thinking. Many of those who made the change later asked to be sent back to the line."

"The real core of the problem here," Barry said, "is the employee resistance to change. As difficult as it might be, they have got to realize that automation and high technology are the keys to our future competitiveness. Employees will strongly resist these changes, but it is a fact that manual equipment will someday be a thing of the past. Better quality, less variation, and more consistent production can most easily occur when technology is used to eliminate the 100 percent inspection and continuous checking of products that are necessary."

Barry continued, "In the end, these labor-saving devices will eliminate expensive and repetitive tasks. Of course, unions will resist these changes. However, what we will need are people who can do a variety of tasks, including making use of several machines, not just one as has been the case here. Unions want you to specialize, to limit the number of things a person can do. They want more people working. Unless we start getting more flexibility from them, nobody is going to be working. We have got to have multi-skilled, flexible people."

"The strike occurred because of their resistance to these changes; plus they simply wanted to see how much they could squeeze from us. They wanted to test their power. They are not realistic with their wage demands. They should be glad to get any wages. We are paying higher wages than other companies doing similar work in our area. They have the idea that we can afford whatever they want. We cannot give more than our competition—more than we can afford."

"When the company offer was presented, it was distorted by the union. Mob mentality and hysteria were the result of their tactics. One employee even told me later that she didn't want to strike, but everyone just got carried away. They all got worked up!"

Objective

Your goal is to get the other person to agree with you. You should explain the rationale supporting your approach. Remember, you are determined that your way will be implemented.

ROLE PLAY # 4

Mike Lance's Perspective

Mike Lance is a young engineer who is a high energy, fast-track type of person. He is single, socially active and has a passion for pool and golf. He, along with other engineers, is responsible for projects partly secured through federal agencies. The office where he works contains a variety of support staff, including Mary Cowen. Mary is an administrative assistant responsible for much of the clerical and office management duties.

Mike's best friend is another engineer named Bob. Together they usually play pool after work and talk about the day's events. Today they really had a discussion. You and Mary got into a serious fight.

For some time you have had an agreement with Mary. The agreement involves a word processor. The problem is that there is only one processor for the whole office. You need to use the processor from time to time, so you had an agreement with Mary to leave the processor in the conference room instead of on your or her desk. This way both of you could use it. It is inconvenient for you because you have to carry all of your stuff across the office from your desk. Mary only has to move a few feet. It is especially inconvenient for you because you often have to run back to your office while working on the machine to answer a call. Despite all of this, you are willing to do it so everyone has an equal chance to use it.

Despite this agreement it seemed that every time you went to use the processor it was on Mary's desk. When you went to use it she would get angry and tell you that she had to have it, but it would just sit there idle. Since she broke the agreement, today you decided it was fair to move the processor. You carried it to your office to use it. When she came over to get it you were talking to your friend Bob.

When you told her you were still using it, she stormed off. In a few minutes she came back and said that she had been timing you. "Absurd!" you thought. She said it had been over an hour. "Who does she think she is!" you asked yourself. Many times you have seen the processor on her desk when she was not using it. You think it is absurd for her to time you. It is not the first time. She is always talking about deadlines as if she were the only person with deadlines.

The personnel director has asked to meet you tomorrow to see if the problem can be resolved. You are certain you need that processor more than she does.

Objective

Your goal is to create a climate to explore differences between you and the other person. Encourage the other person to express her position and then try to search for solutions that accomplish both of your objectives.

Mary Cowen's Perspective

Mary is a young, highly efficient administrative assistant responsible for much of the clerical and office work. She is married, a member of the Parent Teacher Association, and involved in several civic organizations. She works in an office with several other employees, including several engineering planners. One of these is an obnoxious and overbearing engineer named Mike Lance.

You have gotten along fine with everyone else except for Lance. It has now gotten to the point at which he is almost impossible to tolerate. For example, today you had to use the word processor for some important documents that had to be done by the end of the day. Since they involved much indexing, you took the word processor from the conference room to use it. Unfortunately, you have had to share the processor with Lance, so in the past you had agreed to leave it in the conference room, even though he rarely uses it. You think that Lance is always using the processor when he could easily write out memos.

At any rate, when he saw the processor on your desk he came

over, glared, and said he had to have it. You let him have it, but you told him you would need it back to finish the reports you were typing. Later when you went to get it, he was not using it. When you approached him he was talking with a friend about a party they had gone to and about some "broads" they had met. He seems to always be talking like that when you are around.

You asked him for the processor and he said, "I'm still using it!" You asked in a nice way for him to please hurry because you needed it for a project you had to complete. He glared at you and said he would finish in a moment. You knew he was procrastinating and trying to irritate you.

When you went back in half an hour he glared at you again and said he was still using it. Thirty minutes later you went back and said it had been an hour and that you really needed it to finish the report. Then he erupted and insulted you by saying, "Quit timing me. I'll return it as soon as I can." All the time he was talking to his friend.

The personnel director got involved. Now you have a meeting with him. You are sure Lance will want more control of the processor, since he thinks he is the only one in the office.

Objective

Your goal is to create a climate to explore differences between you and the other person. Encourage the other person to express his position and then try to search for solutions that accomplish both of your objectives.

Positive/Negative Evaluation Form

Evaluate each role play in terms of how the interaction made you feel. The number of each round should be recorded either on the left or right depending on whether it made you feel more positive or negative toward the other person. The scale below ranges from "1" (very dissatisfied) to "5" (very satisfied). Place the number of the round you have completed (e.g., 1, 2, 3, or 4) at the appropriate point on the scale.

1. How did you feel about the interaction?

Dissatisfied Satisfied

1 2 3 4 5

2. How cooperative did you feel?

Uncooperative Cooperative

1 2 3 4 5

3. How empathetic did you feel?

Not Empathetic Very Empathetic

1 2 3 4 5

4. How defensive did you feel?

Very Defensive Not Defensive

1 2 3 4 5

5. How manipulated did you feel?

Very Manipulated Not Manipulated

1 2 3 4 5

EXERCISE 3
ACTIVE LISTENING

The purpose of this exercise is to improve the listening and coaching skills needed to successfully resolve complaints.

1. This exercise should probably be completed after a lecture based on the information in chapter 4 or other similar material. You should also emphasize that communication is more than words (see chapter 2) and that sometimes strong feelings are associated with words. Point out that what is sometimes said and what is sometimes meant may be different.
2. Divide the group into pairs of participants. Tell each pair that one member is to act as the employee, while the other acts as the supervisor in the scenarios described in the following pages. These active listening scenarios alternate employee and supervisor interactions.
3. You should give a copy of the active listening scenario and a pencil to each person, then review the instructions. Allow approximately fifteen to twenty minutes for participants to complete this part of the exercise.
4. After this initial twenty-minute period, the same scenario is given to each pair and the participants reverse roles. Now the supervisor plays the part of the employee and vice versa.
5. After the last twenty-minute period, you should reassemble the whole group and give it the answer to the scenario (see answers to scenario). You should then review these suggested responses and be willing to discuss other possible relevant answers.
6. Finally, ask participants to note any observations they made about the experience and discuss those experiences with the whole group.

ACTIVE LISTENING SCENARIO

One should always be aware of the connotative and denotative meanings of words. It is important to look for the meaning of words, not just the words. To do this you need to apply active listening.

Each of you should read the scenario below. To begin, one person acting as the employee will read the first phrase and the other person acting as the supervisor will try to give an active listening response. The next time the supervisor will read the statement and then the employee will respond in an active listening manner. Each will take turns reading a statement; then the other will respond by using active listening. Since statements alternate, one participant is always acting as the supervisor and one is always acting as the employee.

Situation	**Response**
1. Employee doesn't believe management trusts him and says, "I was doing fine before. I don't need you to look over my shoulder all the time."	You respond:
2. Supervisor (who needs a report in a hurry) says, "Looks like we're going to be working overtime if things don't change."	You respond:
3. Employee, when told he has to finish a report by tomorrow, says, "What! I told you the trouble we've had. It can't be finished. This is too short."	You respond:
4. Employees did not volunteer for overtime. Supervisor feels young employees (or other groups) do not work hard enough and says, "People today just don't have any work ethic."	You respond:
5. Employee is upset over job assignment and says, "This isn't right. I'm not supposed to do that job!"	You respond:
6. Supervisor feels the other supervisor's employees are not following the proper job procedures and says, "You guys are going to end up in a lot of trouble. Stop interfering with my people."	You respond:

7. Subordinate who is upset over the merit money she will receive says, "Nobody around here cares about the job you do!"

You respond:

8. Supervisor is upset over production quota and says, "You guys have got to quit dragging your feet."

You respond:

9. Employee feels he has been discriminated against and says, "It's not fair the way some people are treated around here."

You respond:

10. Supervisor is angry about an employee coming to work late and says, "We're behind schedule. It's ridiculous the way everyone treats this job."

You respond:

Possible Responses

1. "You feel frustrated because you are doing a good job?" or "You believe I should trust you because of your experience?"
2. "You are concerned about meeting the deadline?" or "You're probably feeling pressure from upper management to have the report completed."
3. "You feel upset about the deadline?" or "You feel discouraged because the work load is too much?" or "You're angry about the tight time frame?"
4. "You feel discouraged about the lack of concern about the job?" or "You're upset because young people are not as committed to the job as you are?"
5. "You feel irritated about the job I assigned you?" or "You're angry about the job assignment?"
6. "You don't believe we are following the proper procedure?" or "You feel upset over the way we are handling the task?"

7. "You are frustrated about your evaluation?" or "You feel I didn't judge you fairly?"
8. "You're discouraged about the production standard?" or "You are concerned that you might not be able to meet our goals?"
9. "You think you are being treated unfairly?" or "You are upset over the way jobs are assigned?"
10. "You are upset about my coming in late?" or "You feel I have taken advantage of the situation?"

EXERCISE 4
COMPLAINT HANDLING

PURPOSE

1. Discover and share reactions to different ways of dealing with complaints and find new ways of managing complaints.
2. There can be an unlimited number of pairs of individuals.
3. It should take approximately one hour to complete this task.
4. Materials needed include felt-tipped markers and a flip chart or blackboard and chalk.

PROCESS

1. Discuss the need to manage complaints from subordinates. You should emphasize that almost everyone receives employee complaints and that most businesses have developed their own way of dealing with employee complaints. You should also emphasize that by sharing this knowledge with each other, each participant can discover employee complaint handling methods that will benefit them.
2. Tell the participants to form into pairs. Each pair is given the *Complaint Management Booklet.*
3. Inform everyone to take turns responding to or completing each statement in the booklet. Emphasize that they should not look ahead in the handout but instead go from one page to the next. Plan for about one-half hour for this activity.
4. After you call time, then reassemble the whole group. Encourage each participant to describe what he or she learned about methods for dealing with complaints and what new ways of viewing or managing complaints he or

she has learned. You should then list all important points on the blackboard or flip chart.

5. Focus discussion on managing employee complaints. Material in the book or other source can be used as a reference on the subject.
6. After a lecture on employee complaints, the group could be reassembled to role play a complaint situation.

Complaint Management Booklet

You should prepare a handout for each participant. The handout should begin on page one and be prepared in such a manner that participants only see one page at a time. Contents of the handout should be as follows:

1

COMPLAINT MANAGING

2

Read silently: Do not look ahead in the handout, since this exercise is only effective if your answers are spontaneous. This handout contains a series of open-ended statements intended to help you discover and share your reactions to employee complaints. At the end of this meeting, you will also be able to discover ways of dealing with complaints as well as learn from your partner's responses.

The following rules apply:

(1) Take turns starting the discussion. Complete each statement.

(2) This discussion is confidential.

(3) Do not look ahead in the handout and simply respond to each statement in turn.

3

Complaints are...

4

When employees disagree with me about something important or challenge my authority in front of others, I usually...

5

I feel best about dealing with complaints when ...

6

The most important result of complaints is...

7

If I confront someone I care about, I...

8

I usually react to criticism by...

9

I really dislike...

10

I feel most uncomfortable with employee complaints when...

11

My greatest strength in handling complaints is...

12

(1) Recently I was involved in a complaint (explain)

(2) How do you think I did? What was I feeling?

13

I imagine that you resolve most complaints by...

14

I am most likely to confront employees in situations such as...

15

When I think about confronting a potentially unpleasant person I...

16

I occasionally avoid directly confronting someone when...

17

My greatest weakness in handling employee complaints is...

18

By next year I would like to be able to handle complaints better by improving my ability to...

PART II

LEGAL AND ETHICAL CONCERNS

This section contains three chapters that discuss some types of complaints most likely to result in legal problems if mishandled. Chapter 6 deals with various sex discrimination complaints. Chapter 7 is concerned with discrimination based on race, national origin, and age. Finally, chapter 8 discusses recent erosions in the employment-at-will doctrine, which for years has permitted employers wide discretion in dismissal decisions.

The learning exercises and cases contained at the end of this section will serve a dual purpose: they will provide the reader with realistic examples of the types of complaints discussed in previous chapters, and they will provide excellent training tools for the personnel manager. Each case or exercise is followed by a training note that includes suggestions for its use in a training setting. These notes provide insights that the trainer can use to guide the group toward an acceptable solution. There are no ideal or magic solutions to these exercises and cases, just as there are seldom any in real personnel problems in organizations. Their value lies in discovering through discussion unworkable solutions (and why they are unworkable) and in gaining insight into successfully dealing with human relations problems with ethical and legal implications.

6

Sex Discrimination

Amendments to the Civil Rights Act have changed the legal environment relating to women in the workplace. It is important for personnel managers to understand these changes and know some basic steps they should take to insure that all employees understand and comply with the requirements of the law. Failure to do so could expose an organization to employee complaints and possible legal action. In particular, personnel managers need to understand the primary requirements of three forms of sex discrimination: sexual harassment, sex-based wage discrimination, and pregnancy leave.

SEXUAL HARASSMENT

Attorney Catherine Broderick of the Securities and Exchange Commission (SEC) was recently awarded eight years of back pay. A judge ruled that her supervisors created a "hostile and offensive workplace" by granting promotions, bonuses, and other benefits to women who were more responsive than she to the sexual advances of supervisors (Jones, IV, 1988, 10F). In June, 1988, the U.S. Merit Systems Protection Board (MSPB) reported that 42 percent of the females and 14 percent of the males of the 8,523 workers surveyed during 1987 claimed to have experienced some form of sexual harassment (Jones, IV, 1988, 1F). A private-sector survey conducted by the Association of the Sexually Harassed found that 36.6 percent of women reported having been sexually harassed. Of this group, 55.5 percent were black women and 19.4 percent were white. Fourteen percent of the cases the EEOC brings to trial involve sexual harassment. Because the number of such cases diminished slightly last year, EEOC believes that incidences of sexual harassment are diminishing; however, others believe they are increasing but that fewer women are reporting such incidents (Jones, IV, 1988, 10F).

Other recent studies indicate that at least 50 percent of working females and 15 percent of working males have been sexually harassed at work. These incidents result in lowered productivity, lowered efficiency, increased absenteeism and turnover, court awards, and attorneys' fees (Feldman 1987, 17).

These facts indicate something of the magnitude of the problem and reveal that sexual harassment is a matter not to be taken lightly by personnel managers. It is dangerous to believe that it could not happen at your firm. This becomes clear when one understands the breadth of what constitutes sexual harassment.

What Constitutes Sexual Harassment?

According to Title VII of the Civil Rights Act of 1964, sexual harassment is defined as any unwanted verbal, physical, or sexual conduct that is made a condition of employment, used as the basis for employment or advancement, interferes with work, or creates a hostile workplace. More specifically, sexual harassment is constituted under the following conditions:

1. When submission to the sexual conduct is a term or condition of employment.
2. When employment decisions are based upon whether or not the person submits to the conduct.
3. When the sexual conduct has the purpose or effect of

interfering with a person's work or creating an intimidating, hostile, or offensive working environment. (EEOC)

This definition makes it clear that employees must be careful not only of what they do, but also of what they say. An innocent remark may be misconstrued by the person it is aimed at and could then become the basis for a complaint. For example, simply referring to the female members of a stenographic pool as "the gals" could become the basis for a complaint if the steno pool members interpret that as a demeaning term or one that is intended to put or keep them "in their place" (of low status).

The personnel manager cannot limit concern on this issue only to company employees. Sexual harassment can also come from the employees of another company. For example, a repairman or a person who delivers office supplies purchased from another company might make verbal or physical advances toward an employee of the opposite sex while on company premises. This situation is also part of the work environment and thus is covered by the EEOC definition of sexual harassment for which the employer is responsible. If a complaint is registered, it must be dealt with, even though one of the company's own employees was not the one who generated the complaint. An employer can be responsible for the actions of nonemployees when they involve sexual harassment.

HANDLING SEXUAL HARASSMENT COMPLAINTS

In general, the personnel manager can best assist the chief executive by assuring that employees are aware of the issue and its potential dangers and by developing procedures to deal with offenders. The first step is to raise the subject of sexual harassment within the company and make it clear that management disapproves and will not tolerate such behavior. This message should provide some specific examples of types of behavior that might constitute sexual harassment and some common sense ways to avoid these behaviors. In a 1987 survey including 74 responding companies, 50 stated that they had a formal policy on sexual harassment. The remaining 24 are living dangerously, because not having a formal policy in the event of a registered complaint would greatly weaken the company's position on the issue. Of the 52 companies that reported how often they update their policies, 35 percent do so annually, 13 percent biennially, 2 percent every five years, and 17 percent never change. Some of the others do so as needed or have such new policies that they have not yet needed revision. The surveyed companies communicated their policies in several ways, including orientation material, policy statements, newsletters, bulletin boards, training sessions, employee handbooks, memos to employees' homes, and check stuffers. Certainly a combination of methods is possible and desirable (Feldman 1987, 12–13).

The second step is to encourage employees who are sexually harassed to talk about the incidents to company officials. Discussing the problem is important to both the employee and the company's interests: it will help the employees to talk to someone they trust, and company officials need to know about these incidents. Because of the sensitive nature of these issues, a variety of people may be sought out by a harassed employee. Some will not feel comfortable in talking with the personnel manager or other high-level company official whom they barely know. They may prefer to talk to a supervisor or fellow employee. It is important that the harassed persons talk to someone. They can be encouraged to do so by many methods: attitude surveys, hotlines, "speak out" boxes, ombudsmen, open-door policies, handbooks, bulletin board notices, training sessions, union stewards, orientation, staff meetings, monthly lunches with random subordinate employees, and simply oral encouragement to talk with members of the personnel staff. Regardless of to whom they talk, they need to believe that confidentiality will be maintained. Companies have used a variety of methods to insure confidentiality, including maintaining only oral records, providing a written guarantee of confidentiality, and by making no mention of the matter in personnel folders (Feldman 1987, 13).

The third step is to develop appropriate sanctions for harassers.

These could range from a brief suspension without pay for milder infractions to dismissal for more serious infractions. As with any other punitive measures, these should be applied as equitably as possible, and should be accompanied by counselling aimed at making the offender understand the reasons for this behavior and how it can be changed.

Fourth, employees should be informed of their rights under the law. They should understand the legal remedies available to them if they are the victims of sexual harassment and are unable to remedy the situation within the company.

Fifth, methods should be developed within the company to sensitize all employees to the issue of sexual harassment. A variety of means could be used to accomplish this goal, such as films, periodic memos from management citing some actual examples of sexual harassment, and posters occasionally placed in prominent places.

Finally, the personnel manager or other responsible manager should be swift to apply the appropriate corrective action when an offense is substantiated. Quick action will demonstrate the seriousness with which management regards the issue. Just telling the harassers how they are making the victims feel may be all that is needed to end the incident. This was true in the incident that was the basis for the exercise entitled "They're Not Speaking Anymore" in chapter 8. In more severe cases, punitive actions might include a reprimand, transfer of work location, suspension, demotion, or even dismissal (Feldman 1987, 15).

What if investigation reveals that the employee's accusations are false? One can easily imagine how interpersonal relationships between the two parties involved could deteriorate following such a conclusion. The seriousness of the incident and the personalities of the two people involved will help the personnel manager or other responsible executive decide on a course of action. Options include simply having the two individuals discuss the situation (with counselling from the personnel manager offered), issuing warning letters, transferring one of the two, or terminating one or both parties (Feldman 1987, 16).

A checklist for establishing a company complaint procedure for sexual harassment cases is seen below. This list summarizes many points discussed above and will serve as a quick reference to the key considerations in establishing and maintaining an effective anti-sexual harassment policy.

Checklist for Setting Up an Internal Complaint Procedure

—DEFINITION OF SEXUAL HARASSMENT—Include a definition of sexual harassment with clear examples.

—FORMAL AND INFORMAL MECHANISM—Include both:

INFORMAL—Give employees a place to go to talk where they can remain anonymous and no written records will be kept.

FORMAL—Provide a formal complaint mechanism. Then an employee name must be included in the complaint and a written record is kept.

—CONFIDENTIALITY—Victims of sexual harassment—not management—should decide when their names will be disclosed. In the informal process, it should not be necessary to reveal the complainant's name.

—RECORDKEEPING FUNCTION—You can choose to keep a written record of all complaints filed, even those in the informal process. But since an informal complaint (particularly an anonymous one) is only an allegation, keeping a written record of it could be unfair to the alleged harasser who has no knowledge of the complaint and has had no chance to tell his or her side of the story.

—INVESTIGATION AND HEARING PROCESS—A hearing can be held if an investigation does not resolve the complaint. Decide who or what body will hear the complaint and how formal the hearing will be.

—APPEAL—In an appeal, the evidence gathered in the

hearing and investigation is reviewed to see if the decision reached was reasonable.

—TIME LINES—Set limitations on how long each step can take. Also, set a "statute of limitations," the time period within which an employee must complain about the sexual harassment.

—OPTIONS—Provide employees experiencing harassment with several places to complain so they do not have to complain to the harasser or someone with whom they do not feel comfortable. Employees should also be informed of their legal rights to complain outside of the company.

—SANCTIONS AND DISCIPLINE FOR HARASSERS—Include a list of possible sanctions and progressive discipline for any employee found to have sexually harassed another employee.

—PUBLICITY—Inform employees of the procedure through a vigorous in-house publicity campaign including posting throughout the workplace and informing all new employees through the orientation program.

—REVIEW OF THE PROCEDURE—Look at your procedure annually for ways to improve it. Get feedback from employees and managers. Also, provide them with an annual report on the effectiveness of the procedure including number of complaints, final outcomes, and publicity efforts.

Source: Reprinted from *What Every Employer Should Be Doing about Sexual Harassment*, copyright 1986, Business and Legal Reports, Inc. Reprinted with permission of publisher.

SEX-BASED WAGE DISCRIMINATION

Wage discrimination based on a person's sex is another potential basis for complaints. This issue falls under the purview of the Civil Rights Act of 1964 and the Equal Pay Act of 1973. The point of these laws is not that men and women must always receive equal pay if they perform in the same type of job within a particular company. It is legal to have different pay levels for the same job if the pay differentials are based on a seniority system, a merit system, a system measuring quantity or quality, or any factor other than one's sex (EEOC). In the absence of some other justifiable factor, an employee may bring forth a sex discrimination complaint.

There have been cases when an employer has punished a person after a sex-based discrimination complaint was lodged. For example, suppose a female pointed out to her boss or to a personnel manager on several occasions that she was paid much less than two male employees who were doing the same job and who had the same amount of experience, seniority, and about the same performance ratings as she did. The manager may consider the complainant to be a nuisance of whom he would like to be rid. Suppose he then began to give her some very tedious and time-consuming tasks, such as filing a large amount of paper work. This task might prevent her from keeping up with her primary work, and, if continued long enough, might lead to her receiving lower performance evaluations. She may even become so discouraged that she quits the job (which may be exactly what her superior was hoping she would do). She could file a complaint with the EEOC. Such treatment as she received is common enough to have received a name—constructive discharge. This term means that while employees were not actually dismissed from their jobs by their superiors, the retaliation of the superiors took a form that made achieving the job's objectives so difficult that the employees voluntarily quit. If the employees win a case of this type, it is possible that the offending company would have to pay back wages.

Personnel managers should monitor wages and salaries paid to various employees to be sure that there is a valid reason for pay differentials. If there is not, investigation is warranted to determine the reason(s) for the differentials. If there is no good reason, steps should be taken to insure the firm is in compliance with the law—and with good ethical practices as well.

PREGNANCY LEAVE

Suppose that Mr. Brenner, a personnel manager, has called Mary, a secretary in his firm, into his office for a conference. The following dialogue ensues:

Brenner: How are you feeling? Your baby is due in about two months, isn't it?

Mary: That's correct, but I'm feeling fine.

Brenner: It seems that you have been slowing down in your work a bit. Why don't you take off and relax until after the baby comes?

Mary: I'm sure that my work achievements are at or very close to my usual level, and I really do feel fine. Also, I need the money now that the baby is coming.

Brenner: Well, we do need to get someone able to get around a bit better in that position, especially since you have to get up and down so much, so I want you to go ahead and take off. Two months is quite a while, but I think we may be able to hold your job for you.

Mary: You *think* you can hold my job? The company's disability plan states that temporarily disabled employees will be guaranteed their job for six months.

Brenner: That's true, but pregnancy is different than an illness.

In this incident, Mr. Brenner has violated Title VII of the Civil Rights Act as amended by the 1978 Pregnancy Discrimination Act. He is in error on two points of that law: he cannot require a women not to work unless she is unable to work, and he must hold a job for a pregnant employee for the same length of time as for an employee afflicted with any type of temporary disability. Mr. Brenner made vague references to Mary "slowing down a bit" in her job. But unless there is a real decrease in her productivity, it will require more than this casual opinion to substantiate a significant decline in Mary's productivity. If company policy permits, Mr. Brenner should request that a performance evaluation be written on Mary at this time. It might substantiate his opinion. In the absence of solid evidence to the contrary, Mary might have legal grounds to challenge being temporarily relieved from her job if she wants to work.

The reason that a position must be held for a pregnant employee for the same length of time as for an employee with any temporary disability is very straightforward: the law recognizes pregnancy as being like any other type of temporary disability. A company will be afoul of the law if it treats pregnancy less favorably than it treats other temporary disabilities.

Personnel managers must also be sure that any health insurance plan the company has or is considering applies to pregnancy. This too is a requirement of Title VII as amended by the 1978 Pregnancy Discrimination Act. This is not an area where the company can save insurance premium money.

Every personnel manager should become aware of the basic laws governing various forms of sex discrimination in the workplace. You do not need to be a lawyer, but a familiarity with the basic provisions of Title VII of the Civil Rights Act and its relevant amendments can prevent some potentially serious problems for the firm. This chapter has covered the most important of the law's provisions and discussed some very likely scenarios in which a personnel manager might become involved. Measures were discussed that will be very helpful in preventing or correcting these problems. Sex discrimination issues are definitely an area where an ounce of prevention is worth a pound of cure.

REFERENCES

EEOC and the Laws It Enforces. Undated. Video Tape. Capitol Heights, MD: National Audiovisual Center.

Feldman, D. 1987. Sexual harassment: Policies and prevention. *Personnel* 64: 15.

Jones IV, J. T. 1988. Against her will: On-the-job advances promote legal battles. *The News-Leader* (11 September): 1F, 10F.

7

Discrimination Based on Race, National Origin, and Age

The previous chapter pointed out the hazards of sex discrimination. Two other dangerous areas for employee complaints where potentially large monetary damages to a firm can occur are discrimination based on race or national origin and age discrimination. In this chapter, we will see some examples of how these problems can occur. A personnel manager must also remain aware of less obvious problems before they become serious.

RACE AND NATIONAL ORIGIN DISCRIMINATION

Supervisor Jim Wilson (Caucasian), while walking through the company warehouse, sees two of his subordinates, Jack Gorman (Caucasian) and Jose Gonzalez (Hispanic), talking to one another while both are smoking cigarettes. The area where the men are located is clearly marked as a no-smoking area by two signs on roof-support pillars and by a red boundary line painted on the floor with the words NO SMOKING also painted in red just inside the boundary line. The two men, surprised and embarrassed when they see Jim appear, quickly drop their cigarettes to the floor and snuff them out underfoot. After a moment of silence during which Jim looks each man in the eye, he says, "I want to see you in my office immediately, Jose. And as soon as he leaves my office, Jack, I want to see you there."

The following conversation takes place moments later between Jim and Jose:

Jim: I thought you were a good example of one trying to create a better image of your people. You've been doing a good job since you came here two years ago, but this smoking incident makes me wonder if I have misjudged you.

Jose: This is the first time I have broken the no-smoking rule, and I realize I made a mistake that involves safety. It won't happen again.

Jim: To be sure it doesn't happen again, I'm going to give you some time to think about the seriousness of violating the no-smoking rule. You are suspended without pay for three days.

After Jose leaves Jim's office in a dejected mood, Jack comes in.

Jim: Jack, I'm very disappointed in you for breaking such an important rule, one that could involve the safety of our inventory, our warehouse, and all of us who work here. Something else must be on your mind to cause you to do such a thing.

Jack: I know it was a dumb thing to do. I guess the baby's pneumonia was on my mind. That's what I was talking to Jose about. I lit up, and even offered him a cigarette, without thinking.

Jim: I thought it must be something like that. Of course, that doesn't mean we can overlook the violation, especially after the damage done by the fire two years ago. I know it's been rough on you and the wife for the past week, being up with the little one half the night.

Jack: I'll be more careful, Jim. It won't happen again.

Jim: You know you are at the top of the list to replace me when I retire next year. If I had to take disciplinary action on something like this, you could kiss that opportunity good-bye.

Jack: I know it, and I appreciate your giving me a break, Jim. You won't be sorry.

To say the least, Jose is likely to be pretty upset when he learns that no disciplinary action was taken against Jack after Jose was required to lose three days' pay and suffer a smear on his personnel record. Jim, the supervisor, has created a situation that could result in a complaint by Jose that he was discriminated against because of his race and national origin. Title VII of the Civil Rights Act states that "It is against the law to apply unequal treatment for different racial, national origin, or other protected groups when disciplining or firing employees" (EEOC). The two men were guilty of the same offense at the same time in the same place. In the counselling session, Jim asked Jack if there were some mitigating circumstances causing him to violate the no-smoking rule; the possibility of mitigating circumstances was never even discussed in Jose's case. In addition, Jim's comment about Jose's example as one of "his people" is likely to come back to haunt him. Jose may interpret this as discriminatory.

Title VII also states that "An employer's placement practices, recruitment, and hiring procedures must be conducted in an equal, unbiased manner" (EEOC). It is against the law to determine job assignments or classifications based upon discriminatory factors. Suppose that two young women of about equal qualifications and employment backgrounds both applied for a receptionist's position. The receptionist would be the first to greet customers, salesmen, and others arriving at the company's main offices. If one of these two women is black and one is a Caucasian, and the latter is hired, will the black woman be convinced that the color of her skin was not a key deciding factor? She may conclude that there was discrimination and lodge a formal complaint with the EEOC. Even if 95 percent of the company's visitors are Caucasians, that fact still does not provide a performance-based reason—which is the only acceptable reason—for hiring the Caucasian. Suppose this had been an Hispanic rather than a black woman? Could the employer say that 95 percent of the company's visitors are English speaking; therefore, the Caucasian was hired? He may need to show that the Hispanic woman's command of the English language was so poor that it truly represented a barrier to the effective performance of her job. Her merely having an accent would not be sufficient to demonstrate this.

Rules preventing non- or limited-English-speaking applicants or workers from being recruited, hired, or promoted to specific jobs may also be a violation of Title VII. So it would not have done any good for a personnel manager to have written a rule to prevent the Hispanic woman from being hired in the example above.

Perhaps the most difficult racial/national discrimination problem to handle is harassment from fellow workers. Often an employer will not even know about such an incident until a complaint arises. A problem may be generated from deliberate harassment, such as hiding a fellow worker's tools, or ostracizing a worker. In other situations, harassment may be unintended, such as telling ethnic jokes in the presence of a worker with an ethnic heritage.

It does not matter whether or not the harassment is intentional. Title VII makes it the employer's responsibility to take steps to maintain a workplace free from harassment, and the employer is subject to penalties for failure to take immediate steps to eliminate a problem. This means that the employer needs to act quickly to investigate a complaint, even if it may not seem to be a serious problem. Like beauty, harassment is in the eye of the beholder. An ignored complaint may turn into a legal problem.

Summary of Race and National Origin Complaints

The relevant parts of Title VII attempt to insure that no U.S. citizens are denied employment or treated unjustly while employed because they are different from the majority of other employees concerning their race or national origin. Many times these differences are not, in fact, the reasons for differing treatments of individual employees, or the reason for rules governing the hiring, placement, or firing of employees. Yet there have been enough real and alleged abuses on racial/national origin grounds that many people are sensitive about this issue. It is difficult to anticipate the myriad ways that discrimination problems can occur. The best policy is to have rules that cover the most obvious and common types of problems that might occur. Beyond this, one should have an attitude toward people that seeks to treat them equitably.

The next step should be to design personnel procedures based on performance criteria that can be measured as accurately as possible, and make hiring, placement, and promotion decisions based on those criteria. Even performance criteria will not create a complaint-free environment, but it will be more effective than using nonperformance-based criteria. In addition, the personnel manager needs to encourage all employees to be aware of possible abuses of fellow employees' rights on the job. Training employees to avoid harassing behaviors is the best way to avoid problems. Role-playing sessions in which simulated incidents of harassment are acted out by employees can be very effective. Following a role-playing session, the personnel manager or other trainer should lead those in the class in a discussion of the likely impact of the harassment incident on the victim, the harasser, and others in the company. Such a session regarding Jim and Jose's no-smoking incident is presented following chapter 8.

Areas where discrimination can easily occur and where special attention should be focused include:

1. Hiring
2. Transfer or promotion
3. Assignment or job classification
4. Discipline or discharge
5. Any other terms or conditions of employment

Number five on this list can include many situations, so constant attention is critical.

AGE DISCRIMINATION

The Age Discrimination in Employment Act (ADEA) states that "terms and conditions of employment must be applied equally regardless of a worker's age." This law prohibits discrimination in hiring, discharge, and other conditions of employment. The ADEA applies to employers with twenty or more employees.

The ADEA was written in response to changing demographic and social trends in U.S. society. Our population is aging. In 1985, 36 percent of the population was over 40 years of age; by the year 2000, it is predicted that 44 percent will be over 40 (EEOC). In addition, people generally are living longer and staying in better health than ever before. As a result, many employees desire to extend their working years beyond the traditional ages of 55 or 60. In 1986, members of the U.S. House of Representatives and Senate unanimously abolished mandatory retirement at age 70. The desire and the legal right to work to an older age has and will continue to create some blockage in the career paths of well-educated younger workers who expect career advancements similar to those achieved by their parents. The confluence of these forces in the U.S. labor market has contributed to cases of age discrimination.

Sometimes younger people harbor notions about older workers that are not true for all of them. For instance, suppose that a newly promoted, 32-year-old manager believes that his older employees will be slower learners, or that they cannot stand the stress of certain jobs. In addition, assume that the manager also believes that these older employees are more expensive to maintain than are new employees. A review of his firm's records will likely reveal that these older employees are costing the firm more in health and life insurance premiums and that they have earned longer paid vacations. All of these facts translate into higher operating costs for the firm. These factors may lead the manager to consciously or unconsciously embark on a series of steps that sow the seeds of eventual age discrimination complaints or even law suits filed under the ADEA.

The manager may begin to be less patient with older employees than he is with younger ones. He might rationalize this behavior by asserting that the younger employees are not as experienced as the older ones. He may begin to require more from them than from others and then reprimand them when they are unable to meet these demands. He may give undesirable transfers to older employees. When they grumble about these transfers, it gives the manager another reason to make critical comments on their performance evaluations. In the manager's mind, these factors may create sufficient cause for the dismissal of the older employee. But in the mind of the dismissed employee, these events add up to sufficient cause for filing a complaint with the EEOC, which enforces the ADEA.

If the EEOC finds that sufficient cause exists, the agency will attempt to secure a negotiated settlement with the employer. Failing that, the EEOC general counsel will submit the case to the EEOC commissioners to vote on whether or not they will authorize litigation. If they do authorize litigation, the plaintiff can request a jury trial. If the employer loses the case, he could be required to pay damages going back two years before the filing of the suit or three years prior for willful violations. The plaintiff may also be awarded attorneys' fees and the costs involved in bringing the action. During a recent year, the EEOC secured a total of $54 million in litigations; $18 million or one-third of this amount came from age discrimination cases (EEOC). Employers must also remember that retaliation or reprisal against an employee who complains about age discrimination or takes part in ADEA actions is against the law.

Clearly the stakes are high when a firm engages in any form of age discrimination. In addition to possible financial penalties, morale can be adversely affected by a discrimination complaint. Even though employees may not be directly involved, such a discrimination issue is likely to sap much of the productive vigor from the work force. The firm can also lose some of its most valuable and productive workers when managers misjudge older and more experienced employees. Only time can replace the storehouse of experience and wisdom lost when knowledgeable employees are forced to leave a firm for no good reason. No replacement for this experience will be found in any university placement center. The firm could lose years waiting for younger employees to accumulate the needed experience. Of course, they could hire it from another firm, but it probably would be at a higher cost than that spent for the older employees who were replaced.

One might look to the 1989 Kansas City Royals baseball team as one example of the perceived value of experience. Why would the Royals, a team with two young catchers on their roster, pay the California Angels' 41-year-old catcher, Bob Boone, $900,000 for a one-year contract? It is not just the belief that Mr. Boone can play well for at least one more year, it is also the anticipation of what those two young catchers and the team's young pitching staff will learn from him. The way he calls pitches will help teach the young pitchers what works best in various situations. The instruction in the finer points of catching and the casual comments the young catchers will hear while sitting in the dugout beside one of the best ever to have played the position will help them learn more than they could without the presence of such an experienced veteran.

This example of learning from the best has been the model followed by the Japanese over and over again. When the Japanese decide that they want to learn something, they invite the most knowledgeable experts in the field to their country. They excel at baseball partially because they study how Americans play the game. During recent years, they have invited American major league all-star teams to play exhibition games following the World Series. They often have American players as members of their teams, Bob Horner, for example.

Most Americans are more familiar with how the Japanese have listened to our experts in the field of business better than we listened to them. The Japanese, not Americans, created the Edward Deming Award for product quality. In many areas of life, we could learn from the Japanese the value of experience. We can start by capitalizing on the experience we possess within our own companies.

The laws discussed in this chapter apply to the following types of employers:

1. Private employers with at least fifteen employees
2. State or local governments
3. Educational institutions with at least fifteen employees
4. Private and public employment agencies
5. The federal government
6. Joint labor-management committees for apprenticeship and training

As in the other areas of possible discrimination complaints, awareness and prevention should be the watchwords. A personnel manager can most benefit his employer by educating employees about the laws regarding discrimination based on race, national origin, and age. Following education, a concerted effort should be made to sensitize all employees to be constantly aware of how their words and actions might impact others. In essence, you should treat others as you would want to be treated.

AFTERWORD

On January 23, 1989, the Supreme Court struck down a Richmond, Virginia, program that set aside at least 30 percent of the value of city building projects for minority-owned firms. On June 5, 1989, the high court ruled five to four in the *Wards Cove Packing v. Atonio* case against minorities who tried to use statistical evidence to show that they were placed in low paying, less desirable jobs at Alaskan salmon canneries. In *Martin v. Wilks*, the court allowed by a five to four vote for Caucasian men employed in the Birmingham, Alabama, Fire Department to challenge a court-approved affirmative action program to bring more black employees to the department years after the program had taken effect (Stephens 1989, 13A).

Brenda Patterson, a black female bank clerk in North Carolina, filed a discrimination suit against her employer. Patterson alleged that she had been given more work than other clerks and had been called names. When she complained to her employer, she was told that by nature black people were slower workers than others. Finally, she was dismissed from her position. She sued under an 1866 statute banning discrimination in contracts. This law was passed after rumors that black slaves recently freed after the Civil War were being mistreated by their employers. The law is broader in scope than the 1964 Civil Rights laws in that it applies to all employers (not just those with fifteen or more employees) and it provides for monetary awards for punitive damages and for emotional trauma, not just for back pay and reinstatement on the job. It also provides for jury trial and has been a potent weapon in civil rights cases during the past two decades.

On June 15, 1989, the Supreme Court ruled against Patterson in *Patterson v. McClean Credit Union* by a vote of five to four. The justices ruled that the 1866 law only applied at the time a contract was made and did not cover conditions of employment after a person is hired (Savage 1989, 14A).

Many leaders in the civil rights movement are concerned about decisions from the Supreme Court during the first half of 1989. These decisions are considered by some as a reversal in the direction of affirmative action. Some attribute the cause to a new conservative majority on the Supreme Court resulting from former President Reagan's four appointees. Others contend that the court is just attempting to bring more balance to the adjudication of discrimination issues (Stephens 1989, 1A). Judge Kennedy's statement that "Discrimination based on the color of one's skin is a profound wrong of tragic dimension" supports the latter view (Savage 1989, 1A). The important question for personnel managers is, "What do these decisions mean for my company's affirmative action program?"

While the shifting landscape of civil rights legislation is being solidified, possibly for years to come, we can expect many pressures to maintain the direction of the past twenty-five years.

Various civil rights groups that have pursued their particular aims in a fragmented fashion may find ways to consolidate their efforts for a common purpose. Attempts by Congress to draft new legislative remedies to address the Supreme Court's recent decisions are also likely. Given these expectations, it would be wise to continue the path prescribed by most of the legislative action of the past twenty-five years. We recommend continuing to build and maintain personnel programs that will insure equality and fairness for all employees while preserving a performance-based appraisal system. These are compatible objectives if the principles discussed in chapters 6 and 7 are followed.

REFERENCES

Age discrimination in employment: A guide to the law. 1979. New York: Michael G. Cleveland, Vedder, Price, Kaufman & Kammolz and Executive Enterprises Publications Co.

Arvey, R. D. 1988. *Fairness in selecting employees.* 2d ed. Reading, MA: Addison-Wesley.

EEOC and the laws it enforces. Undated. Video Tape. Capitol Heights, MD: National Audiovisual Center.

Hain, H. C., and Sloane, P. J. 1981. *Equal employment issues: Race and sex discrimination in the United States, Canada, and Britain.* New York: Praeger.

Hill, H. 1977. *Black labor and the American legal system.* Washington: Bureau of National Affairs.

Savage, D. G. 1989. Supreme Court limits reach of anti-discrimination law. *The News-Leader* (16 June): 1A, 14A.

Stephens, J. 1989. Civil rights laws at risk after high court rulings. *Kansas City Star* (18 June): 1A, 13A.

Twomey, D. P. 1986. *A concise guide to employment law: EEO & OSHA.* Cincinnati: South-Western Publishing Co.

Weatherspoon, F. P. 1985. *Equal employment opportunity and affirmative action: A sourcebook.* New York: Garland Publishing.

8

Employment at Will

It has long been held in this country that an employee serves at the pleasure of his employer. This is known as the employment-at-will doctrine, the essence of which is well summarized by the following statement from the *Criscione v. Sears Roebuck Company* case (384 N.E. 2d 91 Illinois App. Ct., 1978): "An employee at will relationship can be terminated for a good reason, a bad reason, or no reason at all." (Mackey 1986, 12) This straightforward doctrine has prevailed for many years in the United States; however, it has come under challenge during recent years. The purpose of this chapter is to examine recently recognized exceptions to the doctrine, discuss their implications for personnel managers, and suggest ways to properly handle disputes relating to the doctrine.

EXCEPTIONS TO EMPLOYMENT AT WILL

No federal law governs employment at will; guidance has come from various state court interpretations of particular cases. Thus it is necessary for personnel managers to know how state courts have ruled in landmark cases so they can build a base of knowledge by which to guide their actions.

The exceptions or erosions to the doctrine have fallen into the following three major categories: public policy, implied contract, and good faith.

Public Policy

In general, a dismissed employee may have recourse against his former employer if his dismissal resulted from his refusal to obey that employer's order to violate a public law (Mackey 1986, 19). An example would be the employee's refusal to commit perjury on behalf of his or her employer. The reverse of this is where the employee was dismissed for performing an act encouraged by public law. Filing for worker's compensation benefits or performing jury duty are two examples. Most states presently accept the public policy argument, and their number is increasing (Koys 1987, 574). The public policy exception is the easiest of the three major types to avoid because the issues are fairly clear-cut.

Implied Contract

This is a more troublesome type of exception. Consider the case of *Touissaint v. Blue Cross & Blue Shield of Michigan*. The employer stated verbally to Touissaint that he would "be with the company as long as [he] did [his] job" (Bockanic 1986, 17). The personnel manual given to Touissaint stated that it was the "policy" of the company to dismiss employees "for just cause only" (Bockanic 1986, 17). At first, such language may seem to be motivating to the new employee; however, such words can come back to haunt a personnel manager when he must prove that an employee was not doing his job and when he must define *just cause*.

This kind of problem is not completely avoidable no matter how carefully a personnel manager writes the organization's personnel manual, employee handbook, job application forms, or no matter how thoughtfully performance appraisals are conducted. This is both a blessing and a curse. While the use of key words and phrases has caused interpretation problems, the courts have tended to look at the entire context surrounding a case and not focus only on certain pivotal words. *Mau v. Omaha National Bank* (1980) is a good example. In this case, the court construed that "An agreement to give permanent employment simply means to give a steady job of some permanence, as distinguished from a temporary job or temporary employment" (Mackey 1986, 90). Nevertheless, taking care in wording the organization's key employment documents and in making verbal statements that may be construed as implied contracts is important and will be discussed later in this chapter. Specific wording can be deemed to change the at-will relationship. The following states treat employee handbooks as indicated (Mackey 1986, 72). States not listed here have not ruled definitively on this issue.

Rulings on Employee Handbooks as Employee Contracts

Valid as Employee Contracts	*No Contract Rights Arise*
Arkansas	Alabama
District of Columbia	Delaware
Idaho	Indiana
Illinois	Massachusetts
Louisiana	Montana
Maine	Texas
Minnesota	Wisconsin
Mississippi	
Nevada	
New Jersey	
New York	
Oklahoma	
Oregon	
Pennsylvania	
Rhode Island	
South Dakota	
Utah	
Virginia	
West Virginia	

Personnel manuals tend to be less widely distributed throughout an organization, but usually are available for supervisors and others to read. Employee handbooks tend to be widely distributed to the employees. The following states treat personnel manuals as indicated (Mackey 1986, 77).

Rulings on Personnel Manuals as Employee Contracts

Valid as Employee Contracts	*No Contract Rights Arise*
Arizona	District of Columbia
California	Florida
Colorado	Kansas
Connecticut	Louisiana
Illinois	Massachusetts
Michigan	Oregon
Minnesota	Pennsylvania
New Jersey	
New Mexico	
New York	
Virginia	

Good Faith

In *Fortune v. National Cash Register*, a long-term sales employee was terminated in order that the company might not have to pay him an $8,000 sales bonus (Bockanic 1986, 18). Employees tend to expect that good performance will be rewarded. When the employer tries to find a way to benefit from that performance without having to give the agreed rewards, then a good faith relationship between employer and employee has clearly been breached.

Similar to the above implied contract exceptions, good faith exceptions can arise from oral or written statements made by employers to employees. The legal status of oral promises of good faith is not clear (Koys 1987, 574). This is an area where careful thought is needed to insure fair treatment for all employees. Suggestions to achieve that end will be presented later in this chapter. All situations are not as apparent as in the *Fortune v. National Cash Register* case summarized above.

Other Exceptions

In addition to the three typical types of exceptions we have just discussed, certain classes of employees are protected from the at-will doctrine. Union members commonly have a grievance mechanism to protect them from impulsive dismissals. Civil service regulations provide special guidelines for civil servants. Due process procedures are available to public school teachers, and the tenure system protects those in higher education. If an organization has established a peer review system (see chapter 5), that too stands as a limitation to the at-will doctrine.

The EEOC laws stand out as the most pervasive of these additional exceptions to employment at will. The others are organization- and industry-specific by their nature, and so will not be discussed further here. Personnel managers affected by these exceptions will find the remainder of this chapter as relevant as will those in any other type of organization. The implications of limitations on a management team's ability to rely on the at-will doctrine are equally relevant to personnel policies in all organizations. We will now discuss these implications and what personnel managers can do to adjust to the legal environment the changes have created.

IMPLICATIONS FOR PERSONNEL MANAGERS

Since at-will issues have been interpreted on a case-by-case basis, and since there are no specific laws governing the issues involved, what should personnel managers do to cope with this vague environment? Our first suggestion is to re-examine those written documents received by employees that pertain to the organization's employment practices.

Monitoring Written Communications Received by Employees

Some employers' legal counsellors have advised them to eliminate from their employee handbooks any statements regarding fair treatment of their employees. Some have even been advised to include statements proclaiming that employment is still at-will (Koys 1987, 574). The following paragraphs include some suggestions by authors Condon and Wolff (1985, 16–18) for reviewing your job application forms, employee handbooks, manuals, and other organizational literature.

Remove explicit or implicit statements that *just cause* or some similar term is the only reason for discharge. Such statements invite someone else's interpretation of what constitutes *just cause*. Take care not to write that passing a probationary period leads to guaranteed or lifetime job security. Remember that an informal verbal remark to this effect could be interpreted as a promise. Also, do not promise employment for a specific term. Not only should such statements be avoided, but a disclaimer might be added to the document. The American Society for Personnel Administration has recommended the following disclaimer for job application forms:

> I understand that this employment application and any other company documents are not contracts of employment, and that any individual who is hired may voluntarily leave employment upon proper notice, and may be terminated by the employer at any time for any reason. I understand that any oral or written statements to the contrary are hereby expressly disavowed and should not be relied upon by any prospective or existing employee. (Condon 1985, 17)

This statement may or may not be appropriate for your organization. We suggest that you request an opinion of it from your organization's legal counsel before using it.

It might be wise to add a disclaimer making it clear that the organization's policies are subject to change at any time. This is to protect against an employee claiming to fall under the rules that were in effect when he or she was hired.

Follow to the letter any disciplinary policies you have committed to writing. Failure to do so can seriously undermine your organization's position in court. Make it clear that any list of specific infractions that can lead to dismissal is not all-inclusive. Failure to allow management some leeway in dismissals invites possible future problems.

Any vague language may be interpreted in the plaintiff's favor. Review your documents carefully and make all statements as precise as you can. Be sure there is agreement among the policies stated in your organizational documents. Conflicts or confusion may be interpreted in the plaintiff's favor. Remember that oral promises that contradict your written policies may override them and will usually not lead to the legal outcome preferred by management.

Finally, after completing all this clarification, be sure that your employees receive a copy of all documents regarding employment practices and any subsequent changes to them. Specifically note in your documents any employee group not covered by your written policies, such as union members or professionals working under individual contracts. Establish an internal review mechanism for the inevitable disputes regarding some of your organization's employment decisions. More will be said about this later in the chapter.

We stated earlier that there are no words that can be guaranteed to prevent legal problems or remove all ambiguity from employment documents. Courts will examine the context of a particular case, not just particular words or phrases. While this is true, there is little doubt that the wording of these documents will be carefully considered. For this reason, it remains important to take great care in wording all written and oral communications to employees.

Performance Appraisal

Performance appraisal procedures may be challenged by dismissed employees. To minimize this, keep the appraisals based on job-related criteria and inform employees of the specific criteria on which they will be evaluated.

Be sure that supervisors know how to conduct good performance interviews. Provide them with written instructions for doing so. They should be taught to inform employees of a decline in their performance and to make them aware of any particular event that has affected their performance at the time it occurs. These counselling sessions should be documented for reference in future performance ratings and interviews. Employees should then be given an opportunity to improve their performance (Bockanic 1986, 20).

When the periodic performance evaluation interview is conducted, the supervisor should review the employee's strengths and weaknesses. This is the time to discuss with employees whether or not they have improved upon weaknesses that were pointed out to them in the past. If a Management By Objectives (MBO) program is used, then this is the time to assess the extent to which specifically stated objectives agreed upon at the beginning of the rating period have been achieved. This establishes a firm foundation for granting or withholding rewards since the employee should have agreed to the objectives and how their achievement would be measured. For unattained objectives, the supervisor should offer constructive criticism designed to improve performance during the next evaluation period.

The employee should sign a statement acknowledging that the performance interview was conducted. This will document the interview should any complaint arise later. Before signing the statement, the employee should be asked if he or she has questions regarding the performance appraisal. This is the best time to address any questions that the employee may have.

Finally, the personnel manager should continually monitor the performance appraisal system to insure that it is functioning properly. Changes in products, services, and equipment can bring about changes in the type of employees that are hired and in the way they perform their jobs. These changes can make an organization's performance appraisal system obsolete. It is important to periodically review the performance appraisal system to insure that it does what it is intended to do.

Terminations

Termination of an employee is the primary event that triggers an employment-at-will complaint. The care taken in designing and implementing the performance appraisal system has as one goal the proper justification for a termination decision should a situation arise that requires an employee's dismissal. Any dismissal procedure should contain fair and uniform procedures for just cause. Such procedures are looked upon with favor by the courts (Bockanic 1986, 20). We stated earlier that the organization's written documents should avoid statements regarding dismissal for just cause or other words to that effect. This recommendation still stands. While the just cause statement should be avoided, fair and equitable procedures regarding dismissals should still be instituted, not advertised. Let your actions, rather than printed words, provide the basis for interpretation of just cause for dismissal decisions. Let us briefly review the events that could occur when an employee is dismissed to see why this apparent paradox is sound advice.

Poor job performance and failure to abide by company policies are the most common reasons for dismissing employees. If employees are to be treated fairly regarding these matters, supervisors will have to be trained to be good counselors and good performance evaluators. A worthy goal is to help employees achieve their maximum potential for both their own well-being and that of the organization. This goal involves making the dismissal of an employee as rare an event as possible. To help accomplish this, supervisors should emphasize the connection between good job performance and job tenure. While this may seem so basic that it need not be mentioned, a recent study of many court cases indicates that this connection is not being made in many organizations (Koys 1987, 575). The relationship to performance evaluation procedures is apparent here. It is necessary to make employees think about performance and its relationship to rewards and job tenure. Then if a dismissal situation does arise, it will be supported by a well-documented performance evaluation system.

While the support for dismissal may be documented, it is best not to reveal that documentation to the dismissed employee either orally or in writing. Responding to a terminated employee's questions with specific reason(s) for the dismissal may give the employee's attorney documentation with which to pursue a claim for wrongful discharge. This may seem to be a cold way to deal with the employee in this time of emotional stress, but it is a recognition of the realities of today's legal environment. In addition, supervisors should be instructed not to do or say anything that could in any way be construed as defaming the former employee's character. Idle talk with other employees about the work or personal habits of the former employee can be further transmitted and eventually come back to haunt the organization in the form of a legal claim. Simply put, the less said the better once the employee has been dismissed.

Use of a Dispute Process

No matter how diligent you are, there are going to be some disputed cases that challenge the at-will doctrine. The exceptions discussed in this chapter indicate that the likelihood for such complaints exists. How will you handle them? It is less time-consuming to deal with such cases on an informal basis when possible. But as several earlier examples in this chapter indicate, these situations sometimes lead to legal action. To minimize these occurrences, we suggest establishing a formal mechanism to insure employees receive due process. Brown and Gray (1988, 15–16) suggest several possible forms, one of which may work well for your organization. These procedures are presented here from the most formal to the least formal. All but the first are voluntary.

1. Adjudication. After each party presents its case, a reasoned opinion is reached by a third party whose decision is binding.
2. Arbitration. The parties involved select a third party who

will consider evidence from the contending parties and render a binding decision. The opinions may be reasoned but are sometimes a compromise.

3. Mediation. The two contending parties select the mediator, whose decision is nonbinding. In the end, one party may have to yield to a less-than-satisfactory decision if the issue is to be settled.
4. Negotiation. An informal process in which each party presents its evidence interactively and then the two parties agree on a settlement.
5. Private Judge. The two parties select a judge whose decision will be binding. The degree of formality of the proceedings can vary.
6. Fact-Finding. The contending parties select an investigator who presents his or her report of the facts in the case. The report is nonbinding; it may be accepted or rejected.
7. Mini-Trial. The contending parties select an informal judge and present their evidence. This process is less formal than a trial. The judge's opinion is accepted only upon agreement by the two parties.
8. Ombudsman. A selected third party conducts an investigation and renders a nonbinding report.

It would be best to experiment and then select one type of dispute-resolving process to be used for all discharge complaints. This will help insure that every employee has due process of the same type, preventing possible allegations that a better process was used for one employee than for another.

Recent exceptions show that personnel managers cannot take for granted employment at will. Appropriate steps to preserve the doctrine begin with understanding the recent exceptions the courts have recognized: violations of public policy, implied contract, and breach of good faith. Personnel managers should take measures to insure that their organizations are not subject to such exceptions by examining the wording of all written communications that go to employees, even though courts will examine the entire context of a given dispute. Consideration must also be given to special exceptions granted to certain types of employees, such as civil servants, union members, public school teachers, and those in higher education.

Personnel managers must also monitor their performance appraisal programs. There should be consistency between employees' performance ratings and their career progress in the organization. Supervisors should document specific key events affecting a worker's performance.

These measures should prevent many challenges to the at-will doctrine. Complaints will occasionally arise, however, despite your best efforts. It is wise to have ready an effective dispute process for those situations. Several standard processes were briefly described in this chapter. They vary regarding their degree of formality and whether or not the decisions reached are binding on the contending parties. Each organization should decide on the type that is best for it, possibly through some initial experimentation. You should attend to these matters before at-will challenges arise in your organization. Doing so will lessen the likelihood that they will arise.

REFERENCES

Bockanic, W. N., and Forbes, B. J. 1986. The erosion of employment at will: Managerial implications. *SAM Advanced Management Journal* 51: 16–21.

Brown, D. R., and Gray, G. R. 1988. A positive alternative to employment at will. *SAM Advanced Management Journal* 53: 13–16.

Condon, T. J., and Wolff, R. H. 1985. Procedures that safeguard your right to fire. *Harvard Business Review* 63: 16–18.

Holley, W. H., and Wolters, R. S. 1987. An employment-at-will vulnerability audit. *Personnel Journal* 66: 130–138.

Koys, D. J., Briggs, S., and Grenig, J. 1987. State court disparity on employment at-will. *Personnel Psychology* 40: 565–577.

Mackey, D. M. 1986. *Employment at will and employer liability*. New York: American Management Association.

Legal and Ethical Learning Exercises

EXERCISE 1
THEY'RE NOT SPEAKING ANYMORE

PURPOSE

The following role play is designed for training supervisors and others of your choosing in effective ways to handle a sexual harassment situation. Provide all trainees with a copy of the background section below and have them read it. Then select three trainees and have each of them role play one of the three characters in the incident: Jerry, Ann, and the company's personnel manager. You will find helpful ways to conduct the role play and a related discussion in the teaching note that follows the background.

BACKGROUND

Jerry Cochran and Ann Meriwether were employees of Dack Manufacturing Corporation, a producer of stamped metal nameplates for a variety of original equipment manufacturers. Both Jerry and Ann worked in the Packaging Department, which consisted of thirty-five employees who performed a final quality control inspection of the products before packaging them for shipment.

Jerry and Ann were both single and had been dating each other steadily for about two years. They frequently took coffee breaks together in the company cafeteria, where they were sometimes seen to be touching hands and talking in low tones. The light conversation they exchanged with each other in the department sometimes included little innuendos that made it apparent the couple was on rather intimate terms. The other workers did not seem offended by this occasional conversation, and the productivity of the department and of Jerry and Ann in particular was of high quality.

Neither Jerry nor Ann was a regular church attender, but two months ago her roommate persuaded Ann to accompany her on a one-week religious retreat to another state during Ann's vacation. Ann had not really wanted to go, but she decided to go after repeated urging by her roommate.

Ann's Perspective

Quite unexpectedly, Ann had a deeply moving religious experience during the retreat. After returning home, she began attending church regularly with her roommate and became very active with the Single Adult Sunday School Department. She remarked to her roommate, "I should have accepted your invitations to attend church months ago. My relationship to God is the most important thing in my life now."

Ann continued to date Jerry for about a month after her return from the retreat, but the nature of their relationship changed. In particular, she found that she was now embarrassed by some of the usual comments Jerry made to her on the job. When they were on a coffee break in the company cafeteria, she asked him in a polite way not to speak to her that way around others anymore. He became somewhat angry at this and commented to her that she seemed to feel that she was too good for him now that she had "gotten religion." Not respecting Ann's wishes, he continued to make some of the remarks that embarrassed her from time to time. Her reaction was to try to find something with which to busy herself in another area of the department, thus avoiding the problem. This, of course, was only a temporary solution.

The situation did not improve. Since Jerry became upset the first time she discussed the problem with him, Ann did not bring it up again. After another month passed, Ann felt that she had no choice but to lodge a formal complaint with the department head. She did not want to hurt Jerry, even though they were seeing little of each other socially now. Nevertheless, she felt that she could no longer tolerate the remarks. But even after the department head counselled Jerry regarding the matter, the nature of his on-the-job conversation toward Ann did not change. Ann decided to talk to the company's personnel manager about the matter. As much as she hated to, Ann made up her mind that if this did not produce results, she would file a sexual harassment charge against Jerry.

Jerry's Perspective

Jerry did not understand the change in Ann since she had returned from her vacation. He had always felt very comfortable around her. While he knew they were not in love with each other, they enjoyed a close relationship that was pleasantly romantic. Recently, however, Ann seemed more distant, even though he had no indication that she was interested in another man. He thought that perhaps if he showed a little extra romantic interest in her, she might act a little warmer toward him once again. To assure her that he still cared for her, he tried to say more of the sweet nothings to her on the job than he had before. This seemed to have the opposite effect from what he had hoped. She tended to move away from him and busy herself in other areas, rather than respond the way she used to with a knowing smile. Jerry was afraid that his rapport with Ann was deteriorating. The difficult part was that he did not really know why. The only reason he could name was her recent religious experience. Not being particularly religious himself, Jerry did not know how to handle this change in Ann's life.

TRAINING NOTE

This case would make an excellent role play situation for supervisors. The meeting with the personnel manager could be simulated by using three people to play Ann, Jerry, and the personnel manager. You might try two different approaches in your training sessions to see which one you think is more effective: bringing out some discussion points before the role play or building a discussion around the results of a role play conducted at the beginning of the training session.

Whichever method you use, a major goal is to try to find creative ways to resolve the dispute between Ann and Jerry and prevent the filing of a discrimination suit by Ann. Whenever you are dealing with human beings, there is no one pattern or method that can consistently be counted on to resolve disputes. Remember that once a discrimination charge is brought to the attention of management, it must be handled. Few actions will destroy a firm's case faster than the revelation in court that a known problem was ignored.

In the discussion phase, some participants may suggest explaining to Jerry that he is offending Ann. You may question this approach by stating that apparently the department head has already tried this approach to no avail. Ask them specifically how they would try to make this point to Jerry. You can use the responses to this question to extend the discussion further and use your judgment in following the relevant directions in which it leads.

Another good suggestion is for Ann to explain to Jerry how her religious experience has changed her life. Perhaps hearing this from her will help Jerry to understand the change in her behavior.

Some may feel that punitive action should be taken against Jerry. Ask what type they recommend. You can play devil's advocate with this and other suggestions by bringing out any possible negative consequences of the suggestions you receive. For example, what might happen to Jerry's morale and work productivity if you take punitive action? Are these possible results worth the risk?

You can gain much insight into the thinking of your supervisors as you discuss this case with them. You may also learn that they misunderstand the nature or importance of sexual harassment in the workplace. You will have the opportunity to correct these views in a no-risk training environment.

In the actual situation on which this case is based, the personnel manager resolved the situation by having both Ann and Jerry in his office at the same time. At that point they would not speak to each other, except through the personnel manager. For example, Ann would ask him to tell Jerry that she found his comments offensive (even though Jerry was right there to hear what she was saying). As the personnel manager acted as an interpreter in this manner, Jerry came to realize how much he was really bothering Ann and ceased making the comments to her.

EXERCISE 2
THE NO-SMOKING VIOLATION

PURPOSE

Recall the incident about supervisor Jim catching Jose and Jack smoking in a no-smoking area of the company warehouse. Let us develop a follow-up scenario to illustrate how a potential racial discrimination suit might be prevented. This exercise should work well in a training class with up to fifteen people. A maximum of thirty minutes should be enough to introduce and explore the ideas discussed in the training note that follows this exercise.

EXERCISE

Let's assume that Jose serves his three-day suspension without pay and returns to work. The first day back on the job, he runs into Jack.

Jose: Well, it doesn't pay to forget what you are doing around here for even a minute, does it?

Jack: Uh, no, I guess not.

Jose: Did you catch up on your reading and household chores during the past three days?

Jack: I—well, not exactly.

Jose: Wait a minute here—you're not telling me—you have been working all week, haven't you?

Jack: Well, yes. If you're talking about us getting caught lighting up in the warehouse the other day, you'd better believe I got the law laid down to me.

Jose: You got the law laid down to you! I've been cooling my heels without pay for three days! I wish I just had the law laid down to me!

Barely controlling his anger, Jose goes on his break to the company cafeteria and sits alone with a cup of coffee and his thoughts. After thinking over the situation for several minutes, he determines not to talk to Jim about what he feels is an unfair situation. As far as he is concerned, he and Jack are performing their respective jobs about equally well. He does not think Jack has ever been in disciplinary trouble before, and he knows that he has had no previous trouble. As far as he can see, there is only one difference between Jack and him: Jack is Caucasian and he is Hispanic. Jose has heard that Jack is being groomed for Jim's position when Jim retires next year. He suspects that too has something to do with Jack's not getting suspended. Jose determines that he will make an appointment to talk to the company's personnel manager at the earliest possible moment.

TRAINING NOTE

After explaining the case scenario or letting the trainees read a typed copy of it, a good way to begin is to select two trainees to role play the forthcoming meeting between Jose and the personnel manager. The difficulty the personnel manager will undoubtedly have in finding a way to deflect Jose's obvious direction toward a racial discrimination suit should be very effective in illustrating the importance of never allowing a situation like this to develop. Role playing should create a good atmosphere for discussing with the group how this situation could and should have been prevented.

First, an organization should have a written policy stating the penalty for violating a rule important enough to be expressed by posted signs and a painted section of floor space. Second, the rule should be applied to all employees equally. Remind the trainees what Title VII of the Civil Rights Act says in this regard: It is against the law to apply unequal treatment for different racial, national origin, or other protected groups when disciplining or firing employees. Jack offered the excuse that his mind was on his baby's pneumonia. This is really not an excuse for violating a safety rule. It is likely that if Jose had been questioned further, Jim would discover that he too had some problems in his life, as most of us do. He simply offered no excuse for violating the rule.

It is possible that Jim really did not intend to discriminate. His initial anger and frustration over the violation may have dissipated somewhat by the time Jack came to his office. This is mere speculation, but this suggestion should be introduced by the trainer if it is not introduced by a trainee. The point needs to be made that anger and frustration must be reduced as much as is humanly possible from a counselling session. While disciplinary matters need to be dealt with rapidly, Jim could have instructed the two men to report to him in a half hour. Even this short delay may have given Jim time to gain control of his anger and think about the best way to approach the matter.

Another important issue that needs to surface is that Jack was apparently being groomed for promotion to Jim's position in another year. Jose had heard this. Word of who is in line for promotion tends to circulate once the superior's mind is made up. While not a racial issue per se, this does present another apparent justification for a discrimination charge by Jose. It also raises questions about Jack's judgment and thus his readiness to assume the higher position.

This brief and seemingly simple case will provide a surprisingly rich training experience to help your employees see that prevention is the best cure for a possible racial discrimination suit.

EXERCISE 3
THE ABSENTEEISM GRIEVANCE

This exercise should sharpen counselling skills. It deals with an unusual reason for absenteeism that should provoke interesting discussion and fresh insight into an age-old workplace problem. Allow forty-five minutes for your trainees to read a copy of the background below and engage in the exercises described in the teaching note that follows.

BACKGROUND

Joan Wilkinson was a 29-year-old registered nurse employed at a 200-bed, employee-owned, general service hospital. Joan was single and living alone except for her pet cat, of which she was very fond.

One morning Joan's cat was struck by an automobile and seriously injured. After rushing the animal to the veterinarian, Joan called her supervisor at the hospital and told her that she would not be reporting to work for her 3:00 P.M. to 11:00 P.M. shift because of the cat's serious condition. Her supervisor informed her that this would not be an acceptable excuse and that she at least needed to find a replacement to work in her place. Joan said that the cat was near and dear to her and that she must stay with it. Joan's supervisor succeeded in finding a replacement to work Joan's shift that evening at double pay. She also issued Joan a written reprimand and a three-day suspension without pay. Joan promptly filed a grievance with the personnel manager.

According to the hospital's grievance procedure, Joan first had to meet with her supervisor to discuss the complaint. Since the issue was not resolved to her satisfaction there, the matter proceeded to the second step, which was to involve Joe Metters, the hospital's personnel manager. Joe was intrigued by the argument Joan presented in the interview.

Joan stated that the group of women she worked with were all married and had children. She said the women were always talking about their children and their activities. She said it was not uncommon for these women to leave work for a half hour to run errands for their children, ferry them to some activity, or to stay home from work to care for a sick child. Joan stated that since she did not have a child, she never engaged in any of these unproductive behaviors. Her cat was like a surrogate child, her only companion at home. The cat's injury was the first time she had missed work because of the pet.

When Joe first heard of the situation he did not take it too seriously. Like Joan's supervisor, he never thought that the cat's injury was an acceptable excuse for Joan's missing work. However, after listening to her, he found her argument to be quite compelling. Following the conference, he and Joan's supervisor discussed the matter and reviewed Joan's previous work record. Joe discovered that Joan did have a history of occasional absenteeism. She had been counselled regarding attendance and had received one previous reprimand for absenteeism during her two years of employment at the hospital.

After giving the matter considerable thought, Joe called another meeting with Joan and her supervisor to give Joe's response to the grievance. Joe explained to Joan that he intended to let the grievance stand. While Joan's co-workers may have spent work time talking about their children and being absent from the job because of their children, none of these incidents had ever adversely affected their section. He also noted that none of these women ever had a chronic absenteeism problem. On the other hand, Joan's record did indicate past absenteeism problems and he had decided to let the suspension and reprimand stand.

TRAINING NOTE

This incident was reported to one of the authors by the hospital's personnel manager. All names are disguised. As a result of the incident, some very interesting discussions ensued among the personnel manager and hospital supervisors about the impact children have on the workplace.

Even though the grievance was not resolved in Joan's favor, the personnel manager reported that she was satisfied with the procedure. She was not upset about the loss of three days' pay, but rather about the evident lack of sensitivity to her affection for her cat and about what she perceived her co-workers were doing without being reprimanded. When she was treated as a mature person in the grievance procedure, these ill feelings were reduced and she accepted the suspension and reprimand decision. This is a good example of the value of empathetic listening.

From a group of twelve to twenty trainees, select three to play the roles of Joan, the supervisor, and the personnel manager. If possible, choose a male personnel manager and two females for the other roles, which matches the sexual composition of those in the real situation. Allow them ten minutes to re-enact the meeting between the three presented in the background. Tell them to conduct themselves in the meeting as they think best. For example, Joan can present entirely different arguments, the supervisor can recommend no action, and the personnel manager can remove the suspension from Joan's record. They can do what their best judgment tells them should be done. Following this role play, lead the entire group in ten minutes of discussion. During this time, get others to critique the approaches and comments made by the role players. Provide your own reactions to what they say as you see fit.

Next, select three other people to repeat the role play; however, this time tell them to proceed under the assumption that Joan has a perfect attendance record. Her past absenteeism was cited by the personnel manager as a primary reason for upholding her suspension. See how the role players handle the situation when this reason is removed. Follow this role play by leading the group in ten minutes of discussion critiquing the second role play. Be sure to discuss whether or not the group feels that the rationale of upholding the suspension based on past absences is, or ever was, appropriate. Allow up to fifteen minutes for this discussion if the trainees continue to propose good discussion points.

Finally, discuss whether or not it would make any difference if

Joan were Jerry; for example, how many of the trainees would change their decision about the grievance if the absentee were a male nurse? Ask those who would take either a harsher or more lenient approach to the matter to justify the change in their position. Bring up the issue of sex discrimination. Could they really justify a different decision based on the person's sex?

These role plays and discussions will provide the following benefits to the supervisors who participate:

- They will question some of their preconceived notions regarding acceptable reasons for absenteeism.
- They will think about equal treatment for all employees when resolving complaints.
- They will become more sensitive to others' feelings.

Legal and Ethical Learning Cases

CASE 1
THE BONUS COMMITTEE

The five members of the Materials Handling Department (MH) of Westover Metal Fabrication Company entered the company personnel director's office. They had requested this meeting with the personnel director, Jim Harrison, because they were concerned about the outcome of bonus allocations following the second year of the company's cash bonus plan. The plan had been developed and instituted by Harrison two years ago at the company president's request.

Basically, those employees who achieved better-than-average performance were rewarded in hope that all employees would work harder if they could see that they would benefit financially. Each of the company's seven departments selected five employees to serve on departmental bonus committees. Each of these committees decided on several appropriate performance standards. In addition, these committees reviewed the performance of each employee at the end of each year and made a recommendation to the department head. Then each employee was placed into one of four categories or levels of performance, each of which coincided with a level of bonus pay. The department heads compared the committees' recommendations with each employee's self-appraisal, and then made their own recommendation for each individual. Finally, the president reviewed all these recommendations for the company's 100 employees and made his own recommendation, which determined the actual bonus each individual received. In order to make this process as equitable as possible, Jim Harrison had requested at the outset of the program that each department establish good, challenging performance criteria by which to judge each employee. He then reviewed and approved each department's criteria when the program was initiated two years ago.

The members of the MH Bonus Committee were meeting with the president, Jim Harrison, because of their concern about perceived inequities in this year's bonus allocations. They had sent a memo to the president one week ago expressing the concern that other departments were receiving larger bonuses, primarily because their performance standards were lower and thus easier to attain. They expressed the concern that when the bonus recommendations reached the president he made very few changes in them. The committee had hoped he would either reduce bonuses to other departments or raise them for MH; however, Harrison did neither. After briefly restating their position at the beginning of the meeting, the committee members waited for Harrison's responses.

Harrison: First, let me say that I agree with you that your performance standards are higher than those of the other departments, and I want to commend you for them. I also want to encourage you to stick to them. I hope and believe that as time goes by other departments will rise to your level.

Jerry: But, Mr. Harrison, if we maintain our standards and other departments aren't made to conform to similar standards, we are beating ourselves over the head. We are needlessly forfeiting bonus money that could be ours if we would simply rewrite our standards more loosely, as the other departments have done. Unless you are willing to either reduce the bonus payments to other departments or tell them to get more serious about setting realistic performance standards, it would be absurd to maintain our high standards.

Harrison: I understand how you feel at this time. But I can't do what you are asking because I approved the standards submitted to me by those other departments; they seemed reasonable. I cannot now tell those departments that they must change the standards I have already approved. If you will just be patient, I think you will find that these other departments will see you as a role model. I think they will want to raise their standards to your level, and I am confident that they will in fact do so. When that occurs, the whole company will perform better and we'll all benefit.

As Harrison was unwilling to make any adjustment in the bonus plan's performance standards, the conversation drew to a close and the meeting was ended. After the committee left the president's office, Jerry Evans told the committee members that he would send them a memo in the next few days that would set up a meeting to discuss how the committee should proceed.

Questions

1. Evaluate the positions taken by the committee and by Jim Harrison at the meeting. Do you think the position of either party should be modified? If so, in what way(s)?
2. What do you think will be the effect on company performance and morale if the bonus plan continues to operate as at present?
3. What should the Material Handling Department's Bonus Committee do next?
4. What could have improved the communications in this meeting?

TRAINING NOTE

This case illustrates a matter of great concern to all employees—how performance-based rewards are allocated. Edward Deming, an expert on quality control, has pointed out that it is counterproductive to establish such reward systems because they tend to introduce divisiveness rather than teamwork into the organization. To their peril, American managers did not listen to Deming's teachings on quality control during the 1960s, and many management teams are not following his advice on performance-based pay systems either.

Role play would be an excellent way to illustrate the feelings of the characters in this case, especially if some role reversal were involved. By role reversal, we mean having organizational members in the position to institute a performance-based pay program act as members of the bonus committee, and have a lower-level employee act as company president. This may help to create empathy and greater understanding for all participants. The role play should be followed by appropriate discussion. By this time, an informal mood conducive to a good discussion should prevail. Capitalize on it to lead a discussion of the remaining case issues.

The committee members determined that Harrison was unwilling to alter his position, but some discussants may feel that he should do so anyway. Those discussants should be led to state specifically how Harrison might be more accommodating. Harrison must now act, since the committee members came to him expressing unhappiness with his actions. Those who see some way for the committee members to alter their position should also state specifically the form that change should take.

It is clear from the case what direction morale is taking in the Materials Handling Department. What about the other departments? Apparently they are receiving greater rewards from the performance-based pay system, so they may think it is a fine program. It seems that they have learned how to benefit from the system by setting adequate objectives that are not too difficult to attain. What might be their reaction to Harrison's request that they raise the level of their standards?

If nothing changes, can the discontent be contained within MH? Left unchecked, it is difficult to prevent poor morale from spreading to other segments of an organization since people have to interact with each other. Harrison does not seem to appreciate this fundamental fact of organizational life.

The committee is unlikely to accept as valid his comment that he cannot change standards of other departments that he had previously approved. His own words condemn him here. Earlier in the conversation he stated that he hoped and believed that the other departments would raise their standards to the level of those set by MH. This is a tacit admission that MH's performance standards are in line with his real expectations. This begs the conclusion that he made an error when he approved lower standards for other departments, but is unwilling to admit his error and bring standards into congruence across departments. Instead, he is using the common administrative tactic of correcting a problem over a period of time by less overt means than dealing with it directly. Administrators use such a tactic after weighing the behavioral consequences to themselves from taking the needed corrective action against the organizational costs extracted by a slower correction to the problem. Harrison may have made two decisions here: to have MH truly serve as the standard for performance objectives and not to trade one dissatisfied department for several dissatisfied departments, which might be the result of making the changes requested by the MH Bonus Committee. Many behavioral factors go into making such a decision. Discussion should focus on the consequences of Harrison's choice both to himself and to the organization.

It will be interesting to speculate on what the bonus committee should do next. Several possibilities exist. They may decide that they are unwilling to compromise MH's high standards. Or they may decide not to be the organization's whipping boy (which they seem to think they are) and lower their standards. Taking matters into their own hands in this way carries the risk of affronting

Harrison, for there will be no question as to why the change in standards was made. He may refuse to approve the lowered standards. In any event, others in the organization are sure to know what is taking place, and it will be obvious that a morale problem exists.

The bonus committee may decide to do as Harrison said and wait to see whether or not the other departments will indeed raise their standards to MH's level. Ask your case discussants if they believe the other departments will raise their standards.

It is clear that many basic good human relations techniques are being violated. Obviously the president is not really listening to what the committee members are saying. When he does speak he makes very poor use of the communication process. He was unwilling to empathize and succeeded only in creating feelings of hostility and betrayal. Unfortunately, the president had a preconceived solution before the meeting and never intended to make any changes. His approach made the MH Committee members feel like they were in a win/lose situation—and that they had lost.

It is our opinion that the president should have taken a more conciliatory track. He could have used some of the feedback tools described in chapter 3, like paraphrasing and summarizing. He also could have improved his interviewing and listening skills, but neither of these are going to be effective unless he is willing to listen seriously and, if necessary, modify his decision.

It is easier to implement changes with peers because each is on equal ground. Obviously with subordinates many of the techniques described in the first five chapters can be applied with great success. A supervisor, though, presents a unique challenge. For more information on this topic you might want to review the following article entitled "Survival Tactics: Coping With Incompetent Bosses."

You can gain a wealth of insight about your employees' attitudes toward a performance-based pay plan from discussing this case. What you learn can be invaluable, especially if your management team is contemplating or presently has such a plan.

Survival Tactics
Coping with Incompetent Bosses
D. Keith Denton

How many times have you been outraged at your boss? How many times have you said to yourself, "If I were the boss, things would be different"? How many times have you been denied credit for something that you accomplished? If you are like most people, the answer is "often."

In the course of a career, nearly everyone encounters an inferior superior—someone who may have more power or experience but is clearly inadequate in some capacity. Such a person is a threat to your position within the company and maybe even to your career.

There are many types of these inferior superiors. They may be overly authoritarian, and prevent professional growth and development. Such people prefer to make all the decisions and reduce their employees to glorified "gofers."

The boss may also simply be incompetent. He or she is just "marking time," and has little interest in leadership. This person's department is not going anywhere, and neither are the people in the department.

You may also find yourself working under a supervisor who always seems to be stealing your ideas. You do the leg work and he or she gets the credit.

Finally, one of the worst possible situations is discovering that the supervisor simply does not like you. It seems that he or she has a grudge against you, often appearing to nitpick. You may feel that you get no recognition for doing something well, but that the supervisor is overly critical of errors.

This type of inferior superior may not even tell you what

is expected of you—he or she just waits for the next mistake.

The first thing that anyone should do in this situation is to recognize that it is a common difficulty and one that can be resolved. It is best not to become defensive or try to rationalize the situation away. It will not help to pretend that a problem does not exist. Trying to suppress your feelings won't help either. It will take rational planning and action to change the situation—not hostile reaction.

Obviously, the best solution is simply to get out of the situation. The most dramatic choice is to leave the organization. Most people cannot afford to do this, so it becomes a matter of investigating other options.

Alternatives include dealing with the supervisor, getting promoted out of the job, or finding another position that has greater potential. Given the situation, none of these objectives will be easy to achieve.

Difficult, however, is not impossible, and there are things that can be done. There are at least three necessary, basic skills.

Promote yourself. Every subordinate in one of these situations needs to develop both the ability and the desire to advertise himself. This skill is especially important in a dead-end position.

Begin to think of ways to show others within the organization (i.e., peers and those with influence) that you have talent, ability and desire. Of course, it must be done with taste, but think of ways to display your talents. Talents that go unrecognized will not help you get out of a situation or change a supervisor's attitude toward you.

If you are good at working with people, consider volunteering for committee work. If your talent is organizational skills, try to help other departments or areas keep paperwork organized.

Find out what expertise is valued by your organization and then find ways to showcase that expertise. Never underestimate the value of basic skills. Take advantage of good writing skills, for example, by working for company publications.

If you have hobbies or interests that can benefit even a few people, see if you can set up a seminar to help train employees (and increase your recognition as a valuable person).

The idea is to begin thinking of ways to make others aware of your abilities. This provides you with some job insurance if you have the unfortunate luck to be working under a superior who tries to steal your ideas. At the very least, you might be remembered when an opportunity develops.

Learn to increase your personal influence. The second vital skill is to learn ways of increasing your personal influence—both over your job and among other employees. Do not wait for the superior to give you influence; you may wait a long time. Instead, understand influence and develop a strategy to acquire it.

Influence consists of acquired power, which comes in many forms. There are at least four power components.

The first and most obvious power stems from the organization itself; it is *legitimate power.* The more legitimate power you have on paper the better. The object is to have others recognize your right to exercise control.

Whether or not you have any legitimate power, there are many other types of power that can be used to your advantage. For example, everyone has the *power to reward.*

You may not be able to give someone money or a promotion, but you can provide other things that people want. People want recognition for their accomplishments, a sincere "pat on the back" when their efforts pay off.

They also want someone to listen to their problems or worries. They want to feel free to openly express themselves and to get an empathetic response. All of these and more are rewards you can provide by giving the time to be a friend.

Power can also be derived from the respect people have for you. Some people are revered because of the way people see them. *Respect-based power* comes when others identify with you because they perceive that you have qualities that they respect.

Find out which qualities your peers and leaders admire and emphasize those points. Such qualities might include intelligence, compassion, or association with a respected social, political or religious organization. Do not change your personality or prostitute yourself, but choose to emphasize those characteristics others admire.

Accumulate power through information. The more information you have the better. Supervisors and those in other departments respect knowledge. To this end, make it a point to become as knowledgeable as possible about your specialty. Keep up-to-date, know the latest changes and innovations, and keep statistics and accurate files on information important to individuals and the organization.

If possible, have information flow through you. When people need to know something, have it readily available. The more information you can direct through your office (and in particular through you) the better it will be for you.

Consider volunteering to distribute relevant data to those who might use it. Of course, it is wise not to overdo it. Do not provide useless information or data to those who will not need it.

Improve your communication skills. Publicizing yourself and gaining influence are important skills, but additional skills will be needed to increase your odds of actually changing the situation. Developing and improving communication skills are also beneficial. Often subordinates get in a touchy situation because they neglected this skill.

Ineffective communication is a barrier to resolving interpersonal problems. It can also be the source of conflicts and misunderstandings between subordinates and superiors. A bad situation always gets worse when people do not communicate.

To this end, it is crucial for subordinates to find as many means as possible of communicating. Develop both written and verbal skills. When a problem situation occurs, reason out the options and make productive use of communication.

If a conflict arises, increase the lines of communication.

Do not take communication for granted; state your position—and that of others—clearly. Do not assume. Ask questions, and make sure you know what is going on.

Develop the superior's confidence in your ability. Advertising, influence and communication are always beneficial, but creating confidence is especially important when dealing with one particular type of superior.

When your boss holds an iron grip on all the decisions and refuses to delegate, there is little room for growth and development. Whenever you find yourself in such a situation, remember that it can be changed.

If you want to be involved in decision making, it is necessary for the superior to have confidence in your ability. This trust must be established one step at a time.

Your first task is to make it easy for the superior to delegate. This does not mean complaining about having "no say in things." Complaints will not improve things; they will probably make things worse.

Likewise, appearing as a radical—one who always wants to change things—will not help your cause. Some innovation is good, but too many ideas can hurt your overall chances of getting any ideas accepted.

The "boss" already had plenty to do before you were employed, so be reasonable about what can be accomplished. Remember, one piece at a time and, above all, avoid getting a reputation as a radical.

In order to acquire greater input into organizational decisions, you must provide proof of your ability. One form of proof is to present yourself as a mature person; one who always seems to deliver and has a "can do" attitude. When you make a promise, keep it.

Of course, having this attitude is not enough; you must find ways of displaying it. Report to your superior on what you know. Issue short reports or memos. If possible, write clear, concise reports.

Superiors have more confidence in people who appear well

prepared and, most important, who anticipate problems and reason out the possible solutions. Superiors appreciate problem solvers, not problem makers.

All of these methods will help a superior place his or her faith in you, but the best way to effect change is to volunteer. At first, volunteer for little jobs. Look for those things that he or she does not want to do and then do them.

Even using all these skills will not make having an inferior superior easy. Dealing with an inferior superior is, in fact, one of the most difficult tasks that will ever face a subordinate.

When the situation does arise, it is important to take things in hand and resolve the problem. That means establishing a plan of action that includes identifying your strengths and then promoting them throughout the company. This is necessary if you are to begin to overcome the situation.

Show others, as well as the boss, what you can do. Sometimes a valuable or astute subordinate has more influence on others than the superior.

The subordinate who builds support for him- or herself is the one who is solicited for other tasks and is recruited for other positions. Frequently, an aggressive subordinate will move far beyond his one-time superior.

CASE 2
BONUS COMMITTEE REVISITED

Let's imagine an alternative line of conversation to that described in the case "The Bonus Committee."

After briefly restating their position at the beginning of the meeting, the committee members waited for Harrison's response.

Harrison: First, let me say that I agree with you that MH's performance standards are higher than those of the other departments, and I want to commend you for them. I did not see the inequities you see, because I felt that as I conducted my performance reviews, I applied the standards submitted by each department and which I approved two years ago.

Evans: We believe the standards are the problem. We believe there is a great difference in departmental standards and we don't see how the evaluation process can ever be satisfactory unless you force more uniformity of performance among departments or the standards are made more equal among departments.

Harrison: I understand how you feel. Of the two alternatives you just mentioned, there is no doubt in my mind that nailing down a set of standards that everyone can live with is by far the better one, because it strikes at the root of the evaluation system. Perhaps we didn't get enough cross-departmental involvement in setting the standards at the outset of the program two years ago. But I don't think we need to completely reinvent the wheel in order to correct this. How does this idea sound? Let's set up a committee consisting of the chairmen of each existing departmental bonus committee. They will review the present standards from each department and seek to develop a workable set of standards for the entire company. Obviously, differences in the nature of work performed among our departments will have to be

> considered. When these standards are agreed upon, I will meet with this committee and together we will finalize the standards. If the president approves them—and I believe he will—we will then use them next year.

After some discussion, the committee members agreed to Harrison's proposal. By the end of the week, Jerry Evans and the other six chairmen of departmental bonus committees had met and agreed to the plan. A timetable for returning a set of company-wide guidelines to Harrison was developed and accepted by him.

Questions

1. Is the scenario that occurred in this meeting superior to the one described in "The Bonus Committee" case? Why or why not?
2. No method of handling bonus allocations is going to please everyone in an organization. What potential problems do you see with the method for establishing performance standards agreed to by the parties in this case?
3. What are the members of the newly formed bonus committee likely to learn about Harrison's role in allocating bonuses as they seek to develop company-wide performance standards?

TRAINING NOTE

The scenario of the meeting in this case is certainly superior to that of "The Bonus Committee" case from the viewpoint of the Materials Handling Department's Bonus Committee. The committee has gotten about as good a response as could be hoped from Harrison. He is likely to enjoy increased esteem with the committee members.

Members of the other departments are likely to be less pleased. They may not appreciate being forced into a change in performance standards that appears likely to result in higher standards for them.

It may also be difficult for the newly formed, cross-departmental committee to design new standards that truly take into account the differing nature of the work in the various departments.

Line managers above Harrison may still have to approve the new standards. It is clear from the case that the president has final approval of performance standards.

The techniques for using feedback and clarifying solutions described in chapters 1 through 4 can be used most effectively in this situation. Being willing to compromise, seek consensus, and listen with an open mind is essential to generate mutually satisfactory feelings. In an atmosphere of consensus, interviews can be used effectively to develop decisions that rationally solve problems. Funnel and cone approaches can be used to draw out the necessary information. Open-ended questions can be used to collect not only information but feelings about the situation. Active listening and involving others in the solution may take longer but will in the long run lead to a more satisfactory solution. These techniques are discussed in Part I.

CASE 3
SECRETARIAL FRICTION

James Albertson is the director of an insurance firm's personnel department, which is staffed by twenty-one employees. Sixteen of these personnel are divided among four small units, each having a different set of responsibilities. Four of the other personnel are secretaries, each assigned to one of the four units. The remaining member of the section is Marion Jackson, Albertson's personal secretary.

Albertson was experiencing some pressure to provide his department's input to a new management information system (MIS) that the department was developing. This involved specification of the records, files, and data elements necessary to automate a large portion of the department's data. The task had taken approximately ten hours of Albertson's time during each of the past two weeks. His superior expected him to finalize his input to the new MIS in three more months. Meeting this deadline would continue to take a large amount of his time.

Marion had been assisting him with the MIS project, but he had not been very pleased with the progress that had been made so far. He found that he had to provide her with rather explicit and detailed instructions; as was true of her regular secretarial work, she did not exercise much personal initiative. On the other hand, he was pleased that Marion, a 50-year-old married woman, was extremely loyal to him and that her typing and general clerical work were of above average quality. Nevertheless, he felt that the nature of the MIS project with its rather short deadline required that he have administrative assistance from a person willing and able to exercise more initiative and needing less personal guidance from him. He believed that this would also provide more time for him to manage the day-to-day operations of his section.

Albertson thought that Linda Williams, a secretary for one of the four units in the section, could provide him with the type of administrative assistance he needed. Linda was a young, attractive married woman with excellent secretarial skills who had demonstrated initiative and a desire for more responsibility. She kept the personnel in her unit informed concerning the due dates for reports they were required to write. She was an extremely fast and accurate typist, and a good editor as well. The personnel in her unit often delegated to her the task of writing memos and correspondence, which she always handled in a capable manner.

As a result of her speed and efficiency, Linda often had periods of two or more hours at a time when she had no pending work. She frequently complained about this to the personnel in her unit and to James Albertson. This was another factor that led him to feel that he could utilize Linda as a part-time administrative assistant on the MIS project. She expressed great interest in serving in this capacity because she felt it would occupy her time more fully and be more challenging than the comparatively routine work she did for her unit. She assured James Albertson that the efficiency of her performance would not suffer as a result of the increased responsibility. Linda's supervisor agreed that she should be able to discharge the unit's work even with the sacrifice of time that the MIS assignment would require.

Albertson's next step was to meet with Linda and Marion in order to clarify the roles of the two women. He explained to Marion that Linda would be assuming the responsibilities of the MIS project and that Marion would continue to function solely as his personal secretary. Marion appeared disturbed by this decision and asked if there had been some problem with the way she had handled the MIS assignment. Knowing that Marion had a strong sense of personal loyalty to him and was always concerned that her work please him, he responded by indicating that the main issue was time: Linda had more time to devote to the MIS project than did Marion. As the discussion concluded, Marion told Linda, "Be sure to share your work with me when things pile up. I believe you are taking on more than you are going to be able to handle."

Two weeks later, James was not sure that he had made the right decision. Linda had made significant progress with the MIS work while requiring minimal direction from him, and at the same time, the quality of work she did for her unit had been maintained.

Despite this, Linda did not seem happy on the job. She conversed less with the other employees and with him, going about her work in an almost mechanical fashion. Marion had initiated two conversations with him in the office during this period. On these occasions, she questioned him further concerning his satisfaction with her work and asked him if there were any ways in which he felt she could improve her performance. He tried to assure her that he was not unhappy with her work, but that he did hope she would be able to handle more of the smaller details of the job without specific direction.

Linda burst into James Albertson's office one afternoon during the third week following her assignment to the MIS project. Through tears she said, "I must talk with you!" He took her to a nearly deserted coffee shop on the lower floor of their office building. Beginning to cry again, Linda told him:

> I just can't stand it! Marion never speaks to me anymore. Sometimes I see her whispering to one of the other women, and then they look at me. I'm sure they're talking about me. I know that Marion can't stand me, but I don't know why. I'm just trying to do my job!

Albertson tried to comfort Linda by telling her that if Marion really did have ill feelings toward her, time was often the best healer of such emotions. After talking with her for about thirty minutes, she regained her composure. He told her to take the remainder of the afternoon off and get some rest.

When he returned to his office, he spent some time reflecting on this problem and trying to decide what action he should take, if any. He also wondered about the rumor he had heard from Linda's unit that she was looking for another job.

Questions

1. Is there any way James Albertson could have avoided or minimized the friction between Linda and Marion before it reached the proportions described at the end of the case?
2. What options are available to James Albertson at this point and what are their possible ramifications?
3. Which option do you recommend? Why do you think it is the best option?
4. What do you feel are the underlying causes of the apparent friction between Linda and Marion?

TRAINING NOTE

I was employed as a consultant to Albertson's section during the time that he decided to transfer the MIS project from Marion to Linda. Albertson expected Marion to be somewhat upset when the task was taken from her. He was willing to accept some risk of negative behavioral consequences due to the rapidly approaching project deadline, but the problem developed further than anticipated.

It is practically impossible to know with certainty the underlying causes of friction between two employees in situations like this. True feelings will seldom be verbalized, even in counselling sessions; nevertheless, there appear to be some clues in this case. It often happens that reducing subordinates' work loads for any reason is perceived as a threat to their security rather than as a burden lifted. They may feel as though part of their worth and/or power has been taken away. This appears to be at least part of what Marion felt. The age difference between the two women may have been another factor contributing to the friction. An older employee sometimes feels threatened by a younger, more aggressive one.

There are several options open to Albertson, but as in selecting among several antibiotics for an allergic patient, each of them might produce unwanted side effects. He could transfer Marion to another section. This presumes she is purposely instigating the friction Linda is experiencing. Can he be sure of that? He might first counsel her concerning the matter, but this approach carries a twofold risk. If she is deliberately trying to upset Linda, she will hide her true feelings. If she is not, any insinuation to the contrary, no matter how subtle or inadvertent, is likely to be resented. Feelings could be hurt, and a loyal employee might be lost.

Passively allowing Linda to find a new job is another possible course of action. However, if Marion was indeed trying to get rid of a competitor, this option would solidify her power while the section would lose a very promising young employee.

A less drastic option would be to attempt to smooth relations between the two women and hope that they will develop a better understanding and appreciation of one another. The risk taken with this course of action is that their relations might continue to degenerate and their unhappiness would begin to infect the other employees. It is difficult to hide a problem of this nature in such a small work unit.

If there are risks to be taken you can increase your odds of successfully resolving complaints by practicing some of the techniques described in chapters 2 through 4. In this case, useful techniques include the need to use "I" messages and descriptive words to properly define the problem, and listening to what Marion and Linda mean, not what they say.

Up to this point everyone seems to have made poor use of communication and created barriers to resolving complaints. It is important for James Albertson to de-emphasize the win/lose attitude that seems to exist between Linda and Marion. He should emphasize the common goals they share and find ways that both can share the rewards of cooperation rather than confrontation.

There is no guarantee, but if Albertson emphasizes the point of sharing relevant information and positively reinforces Linda's and Marion's contributions to the section's mission, their attitudes may change. Once he has made as pleasant an environment as possible between Linda and Marion, he can set about focusing on resolving any problems that remain. He should seek solutions and not concentrate on past causes. He needs to find out the specific nature of the complaint and then solve it through consensus, mediation, or some form of arbitration.

CASE 4
SAFETY FIRST (OR WHATEVER HAPPENED TO EQUAL OPPORTUNITY?)

Middle West Fabricators, a large manufacturer of steel parts, began an active affirmative action and equal opportunity program about four years ago. The firm had gone far beyond the legal requirements, not only making special efforts to hire and promote qualified women and racial minorities, but also conducting supervisory education programs considered among the best in the industry. Thus, all supervisors had been explicitly informed of top management's strong commitment to equal opportunity, had received extensive training in the legal and human aspects of discrimination, and had discussed and rediscussed what it all meant for their own jobs and for the organization.

Betty Anderson was one of the program's success stories. She was hired three years ago as a management trainee and successfully completed a demanding training program, which developed her supervisory skills as well as her ability to perform many jobs on the shop floor and in the office. Recently she had been promoted to a supervisor position in the General Accounting Department. Although she was one of a small number of female supervisors and initially had to deal with some male resentment, she was reasonably content with her progress and felt she had a good opportunity for continued advancement with the company.

In mid-year a labor dispute resulted in the union's refusal to work overtime, and it was decided to use the plant's management on the production line on weekends to perform necessary overtime work. (In this plant it was not unusual for managers and supervi-

This case and the training note that follows were prepared by Professor Gopal C. Pati and Professor Darold Barnum of the Division of Business and Economics, Indiana University Northwest. Used by permission. All names are disguised.

sors, including those from the office, to work on the floor when such disputes occurred.)

The first weekend's management work force was chosen from those working on Friday. Anderson was sick on Friday, so she did not work that weekend. When she came to work on Monday, a few people made remarks such as, "Weren't there any soft jobs for you?" "Well, I guess when you have connections . . ." Because Anderson wanted to do her share, she specifically asked Jim Kelly, the accounting department manager, to be sure she was scheduled for the following weekend. Later in the week, Kelly informed her that she would be working on the weekend, and she was very pleased. On Friday afternoon the following conversation took place:

Kelly: Betty, you still plan to work tomorrow, don't you?
Anderson: I sure do! Where will I be?
Kelly: Right here in the accounting office.
Anderson: But all the other supervisors will be working down on the floor!
Kelly: (turning and scratching his head) Well, well.
Anderson: Look, there are lots of jobs in the press shop I can do very well. I worked there for fifteen months when I was a trainee, and I know the equipment. Frankly, I know more about it than many of the floor supervisors.
Kelly: (smiles but looks puzzled) Well, we will see.

Anderson went to work Saturday morning and found a number of assignments that she considered trivial on her desk. She spent the entire day in the accounting office completing these tasks. During the day several people asked her if she was working on Sunday also. She told them she did not know. The more she thought about the vagueness of the entire situation, the more annoyed she became. Late Saturday afternoon Kelly stopped by to see her.

Anderson: What happened, Jim? Why didn't I work on the floor?

Kelly: They don't want any women out there at all. A lot of equipment is dangerous and they're afraid a woman would get hurt.

Anderson: Are you kidding? There are women material handlers working down there!

Kelly: Yes, but they are doing "soft jobs."

Anderson: I don't want a "soft job." I want to work like everybody else. Why did you train me on those jobs during my training period anyway?

Kelly: Don't you like to preserve your femininity? (becomes very defensive) If you want to work that badly, come in tomorrow anyway. (silence)

Anderson really did not want to work on Sunday. However, she felt that the opportunity for women to advance in the company was being hurt by such differential treatment, and she believed that she had to assert herself in the organization if she and others were ever to be treated equally. That evening she received a call from Kelly.

Kelly: Hey, you are coming to work tomorrow, aren't you?

Anderson: Oh, sure. Is there any problem?

Kelly: (hesitating and apologizing tone) Oh, no. I gave some thought to our conversation this afternoon when I was riding home. You know, you were right. You are entitled to work in the shop.

Anderson: Oh, thank you, Jim. Good night.

Anderson reported to work on Sunday morning to the number six press line in the press shop. Just before the job start-up time, Anderson talked to the superintendent of the press shop, Tip Houston.

Anderson: Are you sure my being here is not going to create any problem?

Houston: Oh no, not at all. The bulk of my supervisors like the idea, although they felt that women were not very well prepared for this kind of job. (smile)

Anderson: How about all of those months I spent as a trainee in this department? You mean to say that the things that you guys taught me aren't any good?

Houston: (smile) No response.

The line ran well. Anderson, well equipped with proper clothing, gloves, and goggles, had no trouble and contributed as much as any other supervisor. During the late morning hours the line broke down and the whole crew, including Anderson, was assigned to the twelfth line. Anderson asked the press shop's general foreman, Paul Finch, about her assignment on this new line. While Finch was thinking about what to do with her, one of Anderson's fellow supervisors asked her to work with him. Finch was relieved because he didn't have to make a decision that might turn out to be the wrong one. Everything went smoothly, with the twelfth line getting good-quality production and Anderson demonstrating that she could handle the job. Around eleven o'clock, however, Finch showed up at the twelfth line and approached Anderson.

Finch: I have been told to take you off the press.

Anderson: Why?

Finch: They don't want you to work on the press. They don't want you to get hurt.

Anderson: Who are "they"?

Finch: The superintendent of the machine shop does not want you to be there. He went to Pingloff (assistant superintendent of the press shop and Finch's immediate supervisor) and Pingloff told me to take you off.

Anderson: But I'm working in the press shop. What business does the superintendent of the machine shop have to tell me that I can't work here? What's going on?

Finch: Well . . .

Anderson immediately went to see Tip Houston, the press shop superintendent, and told him what had happened.

Houston: (after hearing what Anderson had to say) Isn't this stupid? I don't believe this . . . Well, it's about lunchtime anyway. After lunch you go back to work on the twelfth line.

During lunch hour Houston told Pingloff to put Anderson back on the twelfth line after lunch. He also told Anderson about this instruction. Anderson went back to the twelfth line after lunch and work was again going on smoothly. Around 1:00 P.M., the safety man suddenly appeared to talk to Anderson.

Safety Man: Come with me. I'll find somebody else to do this job for you. I don't want you to get hurt.
Anderson: (irritated) Hey, look. I'm doing my job. I'm qualified. There's no problem here. I've my safety things on. I'm trained. What's the big deal?
Safety Man: If something happened to you, I'd kill myself.
Anderson: Would you do the same thing if someone else got hurt?
Safety Man: (angry) No, because that's different.
Anderson: How come?
Safety Man: Look, if I can't talk you out of it, I'll have you taken out of the line.

He left the area immediately, but after a few minutes, he came back with Assistant Superintendent Pingloff and a man who had been pulled from another department to replace Anderson.

Pingloff: Ms. Anderson, Tom is going to replace you. I know the risk—I don't want you to get hurt. (Then he put his arm around her.) Come on. Let's clean the sixth line.
Anderson: (blowing up) What's going on around here?
Pingloff: (yelling) Nobody wants women to get hurt. You

can't change this place in a week. If someday we have ten women supervisors, things will be different.

Anderson: What's the difference between one and ten?

Pingloff did not respond. The safety man faded away. Anderson stood there and started reflecting. She recalled how Pingloff had not wanted her to work in the shop from her very first day as a trainee. She recalled what Pingloff said to one of the other employees three years ago: "We don't want any 'broads' in the press shop because there are no beds and kitchens."

Anderson left the line, went to her accounting office, and sat down at her desk. She felt empty, frustrated, and robbed of her dignity. She went to the ladies' room and burst into tears. Around 2:00 P.M. she went home exhausted after working about seventy hours that week. Sadness and a feeling of defeat enveloped her. She thought of many options, including quitting or filing a sex discrimination charge.

TRAINING NOTE

Gopal Pati is a human relations/organizational development consultant to Middle West Metal Fabricators, and Betty Anderson came to him when the problem occurred. He already knew all the participants in the drama, having worked with them for a number of years in training and development, including equal employment opportunity training sessions and management counselling, and he talked with them about this problem while attempting to resolve it.

The Issue

The primary concern in this case is how to implement equal employment opportunity effectively. Most of the necessary ingredients of a successful program were already present at this company: there was a strong, visible, and specific corporate commitment to affirmative action and equal employment opportunity, a good outreach program, well-trained supervisors, and competent counselors. The authors feel that this organization is one of those rare manufacturing operations where a supportive climate does exist in which human beings of all varieties can survive, compete, and grow. Yet, in spite of this, some male managers reverted to discriminatory behavior—perhaps inadvertently—while under production pressure and others did not challenge this behavior. Thus, the issue is primarily one of control: standards for desired performance had been set, but processes for comparing results against standards and taking corrective action need to be present as well. And, as in most control processes, most individuals met the standards without intervention, but corrective measures needed to be present for those few who did not.

In this particular case the equal employment training activities needed to be followed by extensive counselling and control of those people who reverted to prejudicial behavior patterns when in the shop. Just as we have benchmark jobs, we need to identify benchmark people and to exercise especially careful guidance and control over them on a continuous basis. Furthermore, deep-rooted organizational reasons for such behavior need to be understood and conditions modified on an ongoing basis to keep them under control. If this is not done, this small number of deviant individuals can completely undercut an organizational affirmative action plan and involve the company in unproductive lawsuits. Moreover, vertical mobility for minorities and women will continue to be the most-talked-about and least-done-about subject of the decade.

Questions

The trainees might be asked the following questions about the case:

1. *What is management's objective?* To provide equal employment opportunity for all.
2. *What is the basic problem?* In some cases this company's Equal Employment Opportunity and Affirmative Action

Program (EEO/AAP) objectives were not attained because of inadequate implementation and control procedures. This company had a congenial organizational climate and a comprehensive educational program. But here, as in most cases, there were a few individuals who would respond not to expectation but only to inspection. It is necessary that a system be present for monitoring and guiding these people. By *system* we don't mean creation of another bureaucratic structure to monitor the program. Control is an integral part of a manager's job.

3. *How should the problem be solved?* Set up adequate control procedures. Involve top-line management of the organization in the effort. Staff involvement alone will not do the job, and it is important that line management be an active, not just a formal, part of the effort. Use informal, as well as formal, means to communicate to the recidivists that biased behavior is not rewarded in the organization.
4. *What typical problems do women face when entering traditionally male jobs?*

    - Often a small group of vocal "male chauvinist pigs"
    - A lack of female peers to relate to; a scarcity of females with whom to discuss common problems or who can serve as mentors
    - Need for a female to be "head and shoulders" above male counterparts to prove herself
    - Necessity to demonstrate assertiveness
    - Often, a few frustrated "dead enders" who resent and attempt to frustrate all other people's progress, but who use sex or race as an excuse for their behavior

5. *Do EEO/AAP training sessions alone result in equal opportunity?* No. If an organization sincerely wants to assimilate women into nontraditional jobs, it must improve its total organizational climate. Good personnel management in general is needed.

CASE 5
MANAGEMENT PERSUASION OF POTENTIAL UNION MEMBERS

Cahen Mills, a large textile corporation in the southeastern portion of the United States, was interviewing applicants for an open position of machine operator. The company had thirty machine operators in its plant.

The company had in recent months been hearing rumors that the machine operators wanted to form a union, because of inadequate pay for the jobs they performed.

Wesley Hall, the president of the company, was informed of this rumor and quickly told his staff supervisors to try to suppress this intent. He also stated to his personnel director, Arthur Jones, that the vacant position should be filled by an applicant "with no prior record of union membership."

Art Jones tried to recruit a candidate who would comply with Hall's request, but after several weeks the only candidate to possess all other qualifications had prior union affiliations. Jones was very upset about this, since he had a candidate who was suitable except for his union past.

Jones, in his worried state, went to Hall and mentioned the circumstances. Hall flatly refused to even consider hiring an individual with prior union affiliation, even if it meant hiring one with less experience.

Art Jones continued to advertise for several more weeks without success. Bill Swigart (the earlier candidate with prior union experience) noticed that the company was still in need of help and called Jones to ask why he had not been awarded the position. Swigart knew that he had all the qualifications, and that because of the

This case and the training note that follows were prepared by Professor Kenneth A. Kovach of the School of Business Administration of George Mason University. Used by permission.

unique required skills not too many candidates could be recruited. Jones told Swigart over the phone that he wanted to talk to him about the possibility of hiring him for the job; however, he wanted to clear up some matters first.

Bill Swigart came in the next day; Art Jones proceeded to say that Swigart could have the job on the condition that he would not try to organize or bring in a union. Jones said that the company was anti-union and that they wanted no new employees with prior union background. Swigart readily agreed to the terms, since he had just moved into town and needed a job. Jones also stated that he would pay Swigart a higher wage than any of his counterparts if he would refrain from any union activities.

Art Jones was very happy that Swigart readily agreed to his terms; Jones thought that because of this, Hall would agree with what he had done. Since Hall was out of town temporarily, Jones went ahead and hired Swigart at the higher rate.

Several weeks later, Wesley Hall happened to be going over the payroll computer printout sheet when he came across the machine operators' payroll and noticed a discrepancy in the operators' pay rates. He immediately called the finance department and asked what was going on. Hall was told that Jones had sanctioned a higher pay rate for Swigart. Hall immediately called in Jones and asked him why he had done this without prior approval. Jones explained the circumstances surrounding the higher wages and said that his scheme was working well. Hall, still not very happy with the whole situation, called the finance department and told them that as of now Bill Swigart would earn the same wage as the other machine operators.

When Swigart learned of this, he requested a meeting with Hall. Hall refused and instructed the foremen to start writing up Swigart for any and everything they could think of. As a result of this, Bill Swigart later told Art Jones that he no longer was obligated to keep his agreement about not attempting to organize a union among the machine operators. Swigart also told Jones that unless his higher wage rate was restored he would immediately begin trying to organize a union.

TRAINING NOTE

This case introduces a number of issues, but perhaps what it illustrates best is the impact that Wesley Hall's management style and attitude toward unions have on organizational performance.

Two major problem areas exist. First, in his position as president of the company, Wesley Hall's admonition to his supervisors to suppress any union organizational effort sets a precedent for similar behavior patterns among other members of management. Hall's style of circumventing the real issues by resorting to questionable tactics is imitated in the behavior of Art Jones, which demonstrates the impact that management style can have on an organization.

Second, Art Jones's unusual effort to hire the only qualified applicant he has seen compromises the company's legal position. His deal with Bill Swigart is an example of what has long been illegal; it presents the instructor with an opportunity to review the so-called yellow dog contract (in this case, without the actual written contract). In addition, Jones's offer of a higher wage in exchange for Swigart's agreement to refrain from union activities is blatant interference and could certainly generate National Labor Relations Board (NLRB) charges against the company.

The list goes on. The discussion questions highlight some additional issues.

Questions

1. Discuss the impact that rumors can have on organizational communication patterns. Does the informal network have a legitimate place in the work environment? How else might Hall have responded to the rumors?
2. Is Wesley Hall's request that Art Jones hire a new machine operator "with no prior record of union membership" legal? At what point does it transcend that legal boundary?
3. Discuss Hall's attitude and approach toward union affiliation. What are the potential ramifications?

4. Identify the flaws in Art Jones's tactics. What led him to resort to such measures (that is, lack of professional training, ignorance of labor law, leadership influences, etc.)?
5. Did Jones have the authority, either explicit or implied, to hire Swigart at a higher salary level? Discuss.
6. Is Bill Swigart bound by his word to Jones to refrain from union activities? What legal steps are afforded to him at this point, based on the company's actions?
7. How would the NLRB be likely to rule on the various actions taken at Cahen Mills? Discuss possible remedies.

CASE 6
AFFIRMATIVE ACTION AND WHOM TO HIRE

Alex Green, vice-president of personnel at the Hackney Paper Box Company, had to make a decision as to whom to hire to be personnel manager for a 155-employee Hackney Box plant located in Philadelphia, Pennsylvania. At this time, Hackney Paper Box Company had forty-seven small plants at various locations throughout the country. Every plant personnel manager was Caucasian.

The company's corporate affirmative action officer had strongly advised Green to hire a young black woman, June Triss, who had applied. But Green believed a young white male applicant, Bob Young, was better qualified for this position. Green had narrowed the field to these two applicants.

Green's evaluation and summary of the qualifications of the two applicants were as follows:

June Triss

1. Is extremely intelligent but seemed to lack common sense.
2. Has a master's degree in industrial relations from Cornell University and graduated magna cum laude.
3. Has three years experience as an assistant personnel manager at a leading nonunion department store. No union relations experience.
4. Supplied mediocre references from Cornell University and the department store.
5. Is very ambitious—told the plant manager she would have his job in three years.

This case and the training note that follows were prepared by Professor James C. Hodgetts of the Fogelman College of Business and Economics of Memphis State University. The case is intended to be used as a teaching device rather than to show correct or incorrect methods of operations. Used by permission.

6. Has poor personality—informed Green she was interviewing Hackney, not Hackney interviewing her.
7. The members of management group at Philadelphia did not seem to like her.
8. Has stated that she would sue the company for discrimination if she did not get the job.

Bob Young

1. Has three years of college as a personnel major but forced to transfer for economic reasons to a small liberal arts college in his home town. He received a degree in history and graduated in the middle third of his class.
2. Has five years experience as assistant personnel manager in a two-person department in a 500-employee unionized paper box plant.
3. Supplied good references from his college and excellent references from the paper box plant.
4. Has an excellent personality—Green and all members of management with whom he talked at Philadelphia liked him.
5. Is not very aggressive—Green doubted if he would ever progress very far in the company but believed he would be an excellent plant personnel manager.

Both Triss and Young had answered an advertisement in the *New York Times*. The advertisement set minimum qualifications of a college degree and three years experience as an assistant personnel manager. The advertisement did not say what kind of experience as an assistant personnel manager and did not say union relations experience was necessary.

All members of management at the Philadelphia plant were white males. The personnel department at the Philadelphia plant consisted of the manager and a part-time secretary. The plant manager and production superintendent had some experience dealing with the union, but this was primarily the job of the personnel manager.

Green had to make a decision this week, so that the new personnel manager could spend some time with the retiring personnel manager before he left.

TRAINING NOTE

This case is concerned with the problem of a qualified white male and a lesser qualified black female being considered for the same job.

The following questions should be asked in order to stimulate class discussion:

1. What is the responsibility of Green to the company? Answer: To hire the best person for the job.
2. Who is the best person for the job? Answers: Some of the following comments should come from the class:
   a. For June Triss
      1. Best education
      2. Greater potential
      3. Black female (EEO)
      4. A discrimination claim could bring about a court ordered affirmative action program
      5. Had the qualifications mentioned in the employment advertisement
   b. For Bob Young
      1. Better judgment
      2. Much better experience
      3. Better references
      4. Better liked
      5. Better personality

Comments: There is little doubt, in the mind of the case writer, that Bob Young is the best qualified applicant for the job but, if his being hired would result in a court ordered affirmative action program, possibly he should not be hired. Also, June Triss may not be a bona fide occupationally qualified applicant, in which case she should not be hired as she probably would lose a discrimination suit.

There is no definite answer in this case. Maybe neither should be hired and the search continued.

CASE 7
GLOBAL UNITED (A): MELBA MOORE

The Global Manufacturing Company employs over 1,500 people in its headquarters in Cleveland, Ohio. The company has several government contracts and thus is subjected annually to an equal employment opportunity compliance review conducted by a federal agency. The company has an affirmative action program to implement its policy of equal employment opportunity. The government's compliance staff has found the company's affirmative action program to be comprehensive and the company to be serious in its attempts to correct any deficiencies uncovered by the review.

The purchasing department of Global United is responsible for ordering all manufacturing materials, office supplies, and services. The department is headed by the chief purchasing agent, Pete Wilson. Reporting to Pete are five supervisors, each having responsibility for purchasing different types of goods and services. Each supervisor has a staff of several buyers, a stenographer, and a typist.

Most of the buyers are college graduates or have a college background with equivalent experience. The buyers are considered semiprofessional employees and are given considerable leeway in their purchasing decisions. The buyers must exercise considerable tact in dealing with the many salespersons who call on Global.

Under the various provisions of the company's affirmative action program (and as required by various governmental orders), all major suppliers and subcontractors must certify that they are equal employment opportunity employers and that they have an affirmative action program. The purchasing department is respon-

This case and the training note that follows were prepared by John R. Hundley III of the University College Division, Washington University. Used by permission. All names are disguised.

sible for seeing that the necessary certifications are received from each supplier and subcontractor.

However, over the years the purchasing department itself had employed only a few black employees. During an annual compliance review in February, the EEOC (Equal Employment Opportunity Commission) compliance staff pointed out that Global was deficient in employing blacks in its purchasing department. Pete Wilson and five supervisors reporting to him agreed that they would make a special effort to employ black buyers.

In August, Melba Moore, a young black woman, began her employment with Global as a clerk-typist in the purchasing department. She had attended a junior college in Cleveland and had studied several courses in business administration. After a year and a half of college, Melba left school due to marriage. Upon leaving college, Melba went to work as a clerk-typist in the accounting department of a chemical company headquartered in Cleveland. Melba worked for the chemical company for three years before leaving due to pregnancy.

When her son, Jeff, reached age one, Melba decided to re-enter the labor market and again assist in earning the family income. Melba's husband, Bob, was employed as a marketing representative by a major oil company and was assigned to a territory in the Ohio area. Although Bob earned a fairly good income, both Bob and Melba wanted to save enough money to purchase a home.

During her first several months on the job, Melba performed in an outstanding manner. She learned her job quickly and reached a high output level as a typist. Melba formed cordial relationships with the other employees in the purchasing department, and she was very pleasant with the salespersons who called on Global.

In January one of the buyers under supervisor Tom Schmitt left Global to accept a position with another company. After discussion of possible ways to fill the vacant buyer's position, Pete Wilson and Tom Schmitt decided to offer the promotion to Melba. Melba accepted the promotion and was moved under Tom Schmitt's supervision. The company management was pleased that it had been able to upgrade a black female employee to fill this semiprofessional position. Melba thus became one of the few black people to occupy a comparable position in the company, although the company did employ many blacks in lower occupational jobs.

However, after several months as a buyer Melba began to complain to Tom Schmitt about discriminatory actions on the part of other members of the department. Melba cited examples of not receiving telephone messages or copies of departmental memoranda on several occasions. She also mentioned an incident where one of the typists refused to do her work because another buyer had already given her some work. Melba further stated that she felt certain supervisors in other departments were biased.

Tom talked with Melba for several hours, advising her that these incidents should "be taken for what they are and no more—irritations that cannot be avoided in the business world." Tom advised Melba that even Pete Wilson did not receive all of his telephone messages and that this was not necessarily a subtle form of discrimination on the part of her co-workers. Melba told Tom that these incidents were attempts "to remind me that I'm the least important person in the department." Melba further stated, "I'm not important here, so if I'm out a day or so, my work won't suffer—someone else will do it or it'll wait."

After Melba became a buyer, her attendance began to slip. During a six-month period, Melba missed fifteen days. On each occasion, Melba had seemingly good reasons for being absent, but this amount of absence was far more than customary in the purchasing department.

Melba was shaken by the following incident. She invited several of her co-workers to a "home-decorating" party over a weekend. A representative of a home decorating firm planned to display his merchandise and provide Melba with a commission on any merchandise sold as a result of the party. None of the men or women working for Tom Schmitt whom Melba invited attended the party. One of the buyers said he planned a trip on that date. Another buyer became ill several days prior to the party and was unable to attend. A stenographer in the unit decided not to attend since she did not know anyone else attending the party. Even though several employees of the company attended the party, Melba was disturbed that no one from the purchasing department attended. She made it a point to tell Tom Schmitt about this experience on Monday morning and she commented, "This shows again that the whites in this department are against me and don't care about my feelings."

In previous discussions of problems in relationships with co-workers, Melba usually had reacted negatively to Tom's advice. No amount of reassurance or personal counselling had convinced Melba that her beliefs were without foundation. Tom wondered what action, if any, he should take regarding the latest incident.

TRAINING NOTE

This case situation in a large company is significant in its relationship to the overall problems of integrating a work force. The text material of the book discusses the socialization of workers of different races and ethnic origins. Certainly socialization is a major part of the overall equal employment opportunity problem, and the case of Melba Moore illustrates it well.

Blacks tend to be quite sensitive to incidents in their work situations that they consider to be discriminatory in nature. From management's standpoint, these irritations may not be considered race related, but it is difficult to convince some black workers of that.

Melba Moore's fears are heightened by the fact that her co-workers do not attend her party. She states: "This shows again that the whites in this department are against me and don't care about my feelings." How can feelings of this type be mitigated? There may or may not be truth to Moore's statement. But, in any case, she believes that discrimination is involved, and it will be most difficult for her supervisor, Tom Schmitt, to convince her of the opposite.

On the other hand, are Melba Moore's problems more related to the fact that she is personally ill-suited for the buyer's position? Was she given the proper training and counselling by her supervisors before she assumed this very demanding job? Discussion on these questions will usually prove to be quite controversial.

At the end of the case, what alternatives are open to Tom Schmitt? Should he try to counsel Moore again, or would he be better advised to stay out of this particular situation, if he can? This is a most perplexing situation.

Bibliography

Age discrimination in employment: A guide to the law. 1979. New York: Michael G. Cleveland, Vedder, Price, Kaufman & Kammolz and Executive Enterprises Publications Co.

Arvey, R. D. 1988. *Fairness in selecting employees*. 2d ed. Reading, MA: Addison-Wesley.

Bockanic, W. N. and Forbes, B. J. 1986. The erosion of employment at will: Managerial implications. *SAM Advanced Management Journal* 51: 16–21.

Boisseau, R. T. and Caras, H. 1983. A radical experiment cuts deep into the attractiveness of unions. *Personnel Administrator* (October): 76–79.

Brown, D. R. and Gray, G. R. 1988. A positive alternative to employment at will. *SAM Advanced Management Journal* 53: 13–16.

Condon, T. J. and Wolff, R. H. 1985. Procedures that safeguard your right to fire. *Harvard Business Review* 63: 16–18.

EEOC and the laws it enforces. Undated. Video Tape. Capital Heights, MD: National Audiovisual Center.

Feldman, D. 1987. Sexual harassment: Policies and prevention. *Personnel* 64: 15.

Finney, M. I. 1988. A good idea—five years later. *Personnel Administrator* 33: 45.

Hain, H. C. and Sloane, P. J. 1981. *Equal employment issues: Race and sex discrimination in the United States, Canada, and Britain*. New York: Praeger.

Hill, H. 1977. *Black labor and the American legal system*. Washington: Bureau of National Affairs.

Holley, W. H. and Wolters, R. S. 1987. An employment-at-will vulnerability audit. *Personnel Journal* 66: 130–138.

Jones IV, J. T. 1988. Against her will: On-the-job advances promote legal battles. *The News-Leader*, Springfield, MO (11 September): 1F, 10F.

Koys, D. J., Briggs, S., and Grenig, J. 1987. State court disparity on employment at-will. *Personnel Psychology* 40: 565–577.

Mackey, D. M. 1986. *Employment at will and employer liability*. New York: American Management Association.

Mauer, G. W. and Flores, J. 1986. Peer review and employee advocacy in conflict resolution process. *Personnel Administrator* (June): 53–58.

Savage, D. G. 1989. Supreme Court limits reach of anti-discrimination law. *The News-Leader* (16 June): 1A, 14A.

Stephens, J. 1989. Civil rights laws at risk after high court rulings. *Kansas City Star* (18 June): 1A, 13A.

Twomey, D. P. 1986. *A concise guide to employment law: EEO & OSHA*. Cincinnati: South-Western Publishing Co.

Weatherspoon, F. P. 1985. *Equal employment opportunity and affirmative action: A sourcebook*. New York: Garland Publishing.

Index

About the Authors

D. KEITH DENTON is an Associate Professor of Management at Southwest Missouri State University.

CHARLES BOYD is an Associate Professor of Management at Southwest Missouri State University.